# PENN'S PROMISE

# PENN'S PROMISE

## Still Life Painting in Pennsylvania

## 1795-1930

**Paul A. Chew, Ph.D.**

*Editor*

**Russell E. Burke III**

*Guest Curator*

**29 MAY — 1988 — JULY 31**

**WESTMORELAND MUSEUM OF ART**

**GREENSBURG, PENNSYLVANIA**

The exhibition and the exhibition catalog were made pos-
sible by grants from the Laurel Foundation, Pittsburgh,
Pennsylvania, the Alcoa Foundation, Pittsburgh, Pennsylvania, the Katharine Mabis McKenna Foundation,
Latrobe, Pennsylvania, and the Pennsylvania Council on
the Arts, Harrisburg, Pennsylvania, a State Agency.

iv

# LENDERS TO THE EXHIBITION

The Art Institute of Chicago, Chicago, IL
The Baltimore Museum of Art, Baltimore, MD
Mr. and Mrs. A. Dean Bartlett, Pittsburgh, PA
Berry-Hill Galleries, Inc., New York, NY
Mrs. Victor R. Bieber, Gwynedd, PA
Mr. and Mrs. John G. Black, Warrior Marks, PA
Board of Public Education, Pittsburgh, PA
Brandywine River Museum, Chadds Ford, PA
Mr. and Mrs. Lester P. Breininger, Robesonia, PA
The Butler Institute of American Art, Youngstown, OH
The Canton Art Institute, Canton, OH
The Carnegie Museum of Art, Pittsburgh, PA
Mr. and Mrs. Mario C. Celli, Greensburg, PA
The Cooley Gallery, Inc., Old Lyme, CT
Mr. and Mrs. William G. Coughlin, Brookline, MA
Delaware Art Museum, Wilmington, DE
Mr. and Mrs. Ralph H. Demmler, Pittsburgh, PA
Oscar W. Demmler, Pittsburgh, PA
Jerald Dillon Fessenden, New York, NY
Flint Institute of Arts, Flint, MI
Franklin and Marshall College, Lancaster, PA
Irwin Goldstein, M.D., Wayne, NJ
Mr. and Mrs. Bruce Gottwald, Richmond, VA
Indianapolis Museum of Art, Indianapolis, IN
Judy Johnson, M.D., Indianapolis, IN
Kennedy Galleries, Inc., New York, NY
Mr. and Mrs. Frank A. Ladd, Amarillo, TX
R. H. Love Galleries, Inc., Chicago, IL

James Maroney, Inc., New York, NY
Maryland Historical Society, Baltimore, MD
The Metropolitan Museum of Art, New York, NY
National Museum of American Art, Washington, DC
New York State Museum, Albany, NY
Pennsylvania Academy of the Fine Arts,
    Philadelphia, PA
Philadelphia Museum of Art, Philadelphia, PA
Anthony P. Picadio, Pittsburgh, PA
Mr. and Mrs. William J. Poplack, Birmingham, MI
The Reading Public Museum and Art Gallery,
    Reading, PA
Mr. and Mrs. Arthur C. Riley, Pittsburgh, PA
Mr. and Mrs. Wilbur L. Ross, Jr., New York, NY
Mr. and Mrs. Walter H. Rubin
Mr. and Mrs. Robert J. Salvatora, Gibsonia, PA
Frank S. Schwarz & Son, Philadelphia, PA
Dr. and Mrs. Glenn H. Shepard, Newport News, VA
Mr. and Mrs. Alvin L. Snowiss, Lock Haven, PA
Spanierman Gallery, New York, NY
Charles A. Sterling, Philadelphia, PA
Mr. and Mrs. James Stewart-Gordon, New York, NY
Dr. and Mrs. Howard M. Tanning, Pittsburgh, PA
Dr. and Mrs. David Ray Vilsack, Pittsburgh, PA
Mr. and Mrs. Donald D. Webster, Chevy Chase, MD
Westmoreland Museum of Art, Greensburg, PA
Donald A. and Bernelda Winer, Harrisburg, PA

# ACKNOWLEDGMENTS

Our grateful acknowledgments go to the lenders to this exhibition, for without them we could not have presented the history of still life painting in Pennsylvania from 1795 to 1930. Although a list of lenders is published in this catalog, it seems an inadequate indication of our gratitude to those who so generously let us borrow from their collections. Museums, galleries, institutions, and private collectors from many areas of the country have touched us with their generosity and support, and we graciously thank them.

Museums constitute a large section of our lenders; consequently, there are many staff members from various museums who should be singled out for the exhibition attention they have given on our behalf. We thank James N. Wood, Director, Milo N. Naeve, Curator of American Arts, The Art Institute of Chicago; Sona K. Johnston, Associate Curator, Painting and Sculpture, Melanie Harwood, Registrar, The Baltimore Museum of Art; James H. Duff, Chief Executive Officer, Gene E. Harris, Curator of Collections, Jean A. Gilmore, Registrar, Brandywine River Museum; Dr. Louis A. Zona, Director, Clyde Singer, Associate Director and Curator, The Butler Institute of American Art; Philip M. Johnston, Acting Director, Cheryl A. Saunders, Registrar, The Carnegie Museum of Art; Joseph R. Hertzi, Director, The Canton Art Institute; Rowland P. Elzea, Associate Director and Chief Curator, Mary F. Holahan, Registrar, Delaware Art Museum; Richard J. Wattenmaker, Director, Christopher R. Young, Curator of Collections, Registrar, Flint Institute of Arts; Robert A. Yassin, Director, Catherine Ricciardelli Davis, Associate Registrar, Indianapolis Museum of Art; Stiles T. Colwell, Chief Curator, Maryland Historical Society; Linda Bantel, Director, Robert A. Harman, Registrar, The Pennsylvania Academy of the Fine Arts; John K. Howat, The Lawrence A. Fleischman Chairman of the Departments of American Art, Maria Reilly, Assistant Loans Coordinator, The Metropolitan Museum of Art; Charles J. Robertson, Deputy Director, Melissa Kroning, Assistant Registrar, National Museum of American Art; Robert Sullivan, Director of Museum Services, Ronald J. Burch, Curator, Art and Architecture, New York State Museum; Ann D'Harnoncourt, The George D. Widener, Director, Darrel L. Sewell, The Robert L. McNeel, Jr., Curator of American Art, Irene Taurins, Registrar, Philadelphia Museum of Art; Dr. George R. Miller, Administrative Assistant, Theodora J. Reed, Registrar, Reading Public Museum and Art Gallery.

Staff members from various galleries also deserve our sincere thanks for their cooperation. James Berry Hill, Berry-Hill Galleries, New York, NY; Jeffrey W. Cooley, The Cooley Gallery, Old Lyme, CT; David Findlay, David Findlay Galleries, New York, NY; Richard H. Love, President, Bruce C. Bachman, R. H. Love Galleries, Chicago, IL; James H. Maroney, Jr., of James Maroney Inc., New York, NY; Prescott D. Shutz, Shutz & Company, New York, NY; Robert Schwarz, Frank S. Schwarz & Son, Philadelphia, PA; Ira Spanierman, Spanierman Gallery, New York, NY; Lawrence Fleischman, President, Russell E. Burke III, Senior Vice President, Fred Bernaski, Registrar, Kennedy Galleries, Inc., New York, NY. D. Roger Howlett, Childs Gallery, Boston, MA; John H. Frisk, Frisk-Borodin Appraisers, Philadelphia; Daniel B. Grossman, Inc., New York, NY; Jeffrey R. Brown, Brown-Corbin, Boston, MA; Bill Vose, Vose Galleries, Boston, MA; Stuart P. Feld, Hirschl & Adler Galleries, New York, NY, deserve special recognition for their helpful suggestions as well as cooperation with the exhibition.

We are particularly grateful to Russell E. Burke III, Senior Vice President of Kennedy Galleries, New York, for acting as guest curator for this exhibition.

Carrie Rebora, Chester Dale Fellow, Departments of American Art at the Metropolitan Museum of Art, is acknowledged for her preliminary research work on the dictionary of artists. Lastly, a separate acknowledgment of appreciation goes to the entire Museum staff whose constant support helped to make this exhibition what it is.

I would like to take this opportunity to thank certain individuals on my staff who have worked directly with this exhibition, for without their help the success of the exhibition would not have occurred. A special thanks to Regina L. Narad, Assistant to the Director, for her seemingly endless amounts of correspondence and organization of the exhibition and catalog; John A. Sakal, Preparator, for coordinating the loans, installing the exhibition, and assisting in the transportation of the loans; Edward Lytle who also assisted in the transportation of the loans; John Bagley, Jr., Chief of Security, and his security staff for their daily assistance; Richard A. Stoner, Photographer, for his supplemental color and black and white photography for the catalog.

The above mentioned persons and institutions deserve more than a "thank you" for their cooperation. The Museum salutes them for helping us to celebrate *Penn's Promise*, a history of still life painting in Pennsylvania.

Paul A. Chew
*Director*

# FOREWORD

The title of our exhibition, *Penn's Promise: Still Life Painting in Pennsylvania, 1795-1930*, relates to William Penn, the founder of Pennsylvania in 1662. When he visited this great land, he saw bountiful green valleys and rich farmlands, indeed a truly great promise. The painters in this exhibition have recorded some of the beauty and bounty of this great Commonwealth and have given us on canvas the promise which William Penn foresaw. The date 1795 was chosen to document the historic Columbianum exposition of May 22, 1795 in Philadelphia. This exhibition was the first public display of art held in the new world and was organized to further the cause of the fine arts. More importantly this inaugural event introduced still life painting in America. The famous Philadelphia artist, Charles Willson Peale, did not exhibit a still life in the exposition, but sent his remarkable *Staircase Group*, (Philadelphia Museum of Art). This work presents the artist's young son Raphaelle posed as an artist with palette and maulstick on a staircase with his brother Titian. Raphaelle was the best represented member of the Peale family in the Columbianum. The 22-year-old artist exhibited five portraits and another eight paintings, most of which were probably still lifes. The year 1930 seemed to be the logical termination date for this survey of still life painting as a theme exhibition. About this time the appeal of the avant-garde of non-figurative and abstract expressionism entered the mainstream of American art. It then became apparent that thematic consideration lost much of its meaning.

Still life, or as the French defined it, *nature morte,* is a painting of a group of inanimate objects, usually dead, such as fruit, dead fish, a bouquet of flowers, or common household objects. The Egyptians represented still lifes of food in tombs. Perhaps the first people to paint pure still lifes were the ancient Greeks. With the excavation of Herculaneum and Pompeii, we have tangible proof of the Romans use of still life as part of their house decorations in fresco and mosaic.

During the Middle Ages, the attention to still life all but disappears. Hugo van der Goes, a late Gothic Flemish artist, includes a still life with his beautiful and famous vase of flowers seen in *The Portinari Altarpiece,* ca. 1476. The interest in still life, although sparce, continues through the sixteenth and seventeenth centuries in Flan-

ders and Holland. By this time, it was being introduced in England. Sir Joshua Reynolds, in his *Discourses on Art* (1770), places the practice of still life painting very low for students, in the ranking of suitable subjects.

American Colonial artists, thoroughly aligned with the traditional English school, also neglected the still life as a thematic consideration. It does appear, however, as a decorative device in portrait painting.

The Colonial painter, Charles Willson Peale, founder of the Peale Dynasty, used still life as an accessory in his portraits. Raphaelle Peale, his son, and James Peale, the artist's brother, are given credit for establishing pure still life painting in America.

Nearly 100 museums, private collectors, and galleries were invited to participate in this important and scholarly exhibition. While the response in general was quite enthusiastic, a number of loans were unavailable for reasons of lending schedules, condition of the paintings, or donor restriction. Nonetheless we can boast 64 lenders to the exhibition, including 19 museums, 37 private collectors, and seven galleries for a total of 116 paintings by 56 artists. We are pleased that 22 of these works are from our own collection.

It must be noted that the exhibition intended to survey still life painting in Pennsylvania from 1795 to 1930; however, admittedly a small number of important artists are not represented for reasons mentioned above, but those who are are the most influential artists who contributed to the rich history of still life painting in the Commonwealth.

Westmoreland Museum of Art is proud to present to the public *Penn's Promise: Still Life Painting in Pennsylvania, 1795-1930*, the third most important exhibition in the Museum's history. To the best of our knowledge, the history of still life painting in Pennsylvania has never been presented as an exhibition or as a publication. The dictionary of artists, which appears at the back of the exhibition catalog, will hopefully serve as research information to students and collectors interested in this area of painting. The exhibition continues our commitment to exhibiting and collecting the art of Pennsylvania.

P.A.C.

# CATALOGUE OF THE EXHIBITION

*All of the paintings are illustrated in either color or black and white following the catalog listing.*

ATKINSON, Jacob (1864-1938)

1. *Souvenir of the Columbian Exposition*, 1893
   Oil on canvas, 12 × 16 inches
   Signed and dated lower right: Jacob Atkinson 1893
   Collection of Indianapolis Museum of Art, James E.
   Roberts and Martha Delzell Memorial Funds,
   Indianapolis, IN

AUSTRIAN, Ben (1870-1921)

2. *Hanging Game (Two Ducks)*, 1909
   Oil on canvas, 28 × 20 inches
   Signed and dated lower right: Ben Austrian 1909
   Collection of Lester and Barbara Breininger,
   Robesonia, PA

3. *Hanging Game (Three Ducks)*, 1909
   Oil on canvas, 28 × 20 inches
   Signed and dated lower right: Ben Austrian 1909
   Collection of Lester and Barbara Breininger,
   Robesonia, PA

4. *The Paper Rack*
   Oil on canvas, 16 7/8 × 12 inches
   Signed on letter: Mr. Ben Austrian
   Private Collection

AVINOFF, Andre (1884-1949)

5. *Dutch Floral Arrangement*
   Watercolor, 21 1/2 × 16 inches
   Signed lower right: A. Avinoff
   Private Collection

BEAUX, Cecilia (1855-1942)

6. *Still Life with Fruit*, ca. 1918
   Oil on canvas, 24 1/4 × 18 inches
   Signed lower left: C B
   Collection of Westmoreland Museum of Art, Gift of the
   Women's Committee, Greensburg, PA

BECK, Henry Kepple (1862-1937)

7. *Still Life*
   Oil on wood panel, 9 1/2 × 15 inches
   Signed lower right: H. K. Beck
   Collection of Donald A. and Bernelda Winer,
   Harrisburg, PA

BIRCH, Thomas (1779-1851)

8. *Still Life*
   Oil on canvas, 17 × 20 inches
   Signed lower right: Tho Birch
   Collection of Mrs. Victor R. Bieber, Gwynedd, PA

BLYTHE, David Gilmour (1815-1865)

9. *Old Age*, 1865
   Oil on canvas, 8 × 12 inches
   Signed lower left: Blythe
   Collection of Dr. and Mrs. David Ray Vilsack,
   Pittsburgh, PA

10. *Youth*, 1865
    Oil on canvas, 8 × 12 inches
    Signed lower left: Blythe
    Collection of Dr. and Mrs. David Ray Vilsack,
    Pittsburgh, PA

BRECKENRIDGE, Hugh Henry (1870-1937)

11. *The Flower Garden*, ca. 1906
    Oil on canvas, 25 × 30 inches
    Signed lower left center: Hugh H. Breckenridge
    Private Collection (Through the Courtesy of R. H. Love
    Galleries, Inc., Chicago, IL)

BRIDGES, Fidelia (1835-1923)

12. *Still Life with Robin's Nest*, 1863
    Oil on wood panel, 8 × 6 1/2 inches
    Signed and dated lower right: F. Bridges 1863
    Collection of The Art Institute of Chicago, Restricted,
    Gift of Charles C. Haffner, III, Chicago, IL

COPE, George (1855-1929)

13. *Civil War Accoutrements*, 1887
    Oil on canvas, 50 × 36 1/2 inches
    Signed and dated lower right: Geo. Cope 1887
    Collection of Frank S. Schwarz & Son, Philadelphia, PA

14. *Indian Relics*, 1891
    Oil on canvas, 30 1/4 × 22 inches
    Signed and dated lower right: Geo. Cope. 91
    Collection of Brandywine River Museum, Museum
    Volunteers' Purchase Fund, 1977, Chadds Ford, PA

DEMMLER, Fred A. (1888-1918)

15. *Still Life with Pineapple*
    Oil on canvas, 18 7/8 × 13 7/8 inches
    Not signed, not dated
    Collection of Mr. and Mrs. Ralph H. Demmler,
    Pittsburgh, PA

16. *Still Life with Violin*, ca. 1909
    Oil on canvas, 18 × 26 1/2 inches
    Not signed, not dated
    Collection of Oscar W. Demmler, Pittsburgh, PA

DEMUTH, Charles (1883-1935)

17. *Cyclamen*, 1905
    Watercolor on paper, 10 1/2 × 8 inches
    Signed and dated lower right: C. Demuth 1905
    Collection of The Canton Art Institute, Gift of Ralph L.
    Wilson, Canton, OH

18. *Daffodils*, 1928
    Watercolor, 17 1/2 × 11 1/2 inches
    Not signed, not dated
    Collection of Mr. and Mrs. Bruce Gottwald,
    Richmond, VA

19. *Tiger Lilies*, 1920
    Watercolor on paper, 18 1/4 × 12 inches
    Signed and dated lower left: C Demuth 1920
    Collection of Mr. and Mrs. Frank A. Ladd, Amarillo, TX

1

20. *Zinnia Bouquet*, 1925
   Watercolor, $13^5/8 \times 11^1/8$ inches
   Signed and dated lower center: C.D- 1925
   Collection of Kennedy Galleries, Inc., New York, NY

EAKINS, Susan MacDowell (1852-1938)

21. *Still Life with Figure*
   Oil on canvas, $28 \times 21^1/2$ inches
   Not signed, not dated
   Collection of Westmoreland Museum of Art, Gift of Mr.
   and Mrs. Stuart P. Feld, Greensburg, PA

FOERSTER, Emil (1822-1906)

22. *Still Life with Peach, Grapes, and Plum*, 1863
   Oil on board, $10^1/2 \times 13^1/2$ inches
   Initialled and dated lower right: E F 63
   Collection of Anthony P. Picadio, Pittsburgh, PA

FRANCIS, John F. (1808-1886)

23. *An Abundance of Fruit*
   Oil on canvas, $25 \times 30$ inches
   Signed lower right: Francis Pt
   Collection of Spanierman Gallery, New York, NY

24. *Fruit and Wine*, 1858
   Oil on canvas, $25 \times 30$ inches
   Signed and dated lower right: J F Francis pt 1858
   Collection of Westmoreland Museum of Art,
   Anonymous Gift, Greensburg, PA

25. *Still Life: A Luncheon Table*, 1852
   Oil on canvas, $25 \times 30$ inches
   Signed and dated lower right: J. F Francis pt 1852
   Private Collection

GLACKENS, William (1870-1938)

26. *Still Life with Three Glasses*
   Oil on canvas, $20 \times 29$ inches
   Signed lower left: W. Glackens
   Collection of The Butler Institute of American Art,
   Youngstown, OH

GORSON, Aaron Henry (1872-1933)

27. *Still Life: Two Oranges*
   Oil on canvas, $8 \times 11$ inches
   Signed lower left: A H Gorson
   Collection of Kennedy Galleries, Inc., New York, NY

HAILMAN, Johanna Knowles Woodwell (1871-1958)

28. *Flowers*, ca. 1920
   Oil on masonite, $20 \times 25$ inches
   Not signed, not dated
   Collection of Westmoreland Museum of Art, Director's
   Discretionary Fund, Greensburg, PA

HARNETT, William Michael (1848-1892)

29. *After the Hunt (3rd Version)*, 1884
   Oil on canvas, $55 \times 40$ inches
   Monogrammed and dated lower left:
   WMH(monogram)arnett Munchin 1884
   Collection of The Butler Institute of American Art,
   Youngstown, OH

2

30. *The Artist's Letter Rack*, 1879
   Oil on canvas, $30 \times 25$ inches
   Monogrammed and dated upper left:
   WMH(monogram)arnett 1879
   Collection of The Metropolitan Museum of Art, Morris
   K. Jesup Fund, 1966, New York, NY

31. *Philadelphia Public Ledger*, 1880
   Oil on canvas, $10 \times 14$ inches
   Monogrammed and dated lower left:
   WMH(monogram)arnett 1880
   Collection of Westmoreland Museum of Art,
   Anonymous Donor, by Exchange, Greensburg, PA

32. *Shinplaster with Exhibition Label and Newspaper
   Clipping*, 1879
   Oil on canvas, $6^1/2 \times 4^1/2$ inches
   Monogrammed and dated lower right:
   WHM(monogram)arnett 1879
   Private Collection

33. *Still Life*, 1875
   Oil on canvas, $18 \times 26^1/4$ inches
   Monogrammed and dated lower left:
   WMH(monogram)arnett 1875
   Collection of The Reading Public Museum and Art
   Gallery, Reading, PA

34. *Still Life with a Letter to Mr. Lask*, 1879
   Oil on canvas, $9 \times 12$ inches
   Monogrammed and dated lower right:
   WMH(monogram)arnett 1879
   Collection of Kennedy Galleries, Inc., New York, NY

HEADE, Martin Johnson (1819-1904)

35. *Cherokee Roses in a Glass*
   Oil on canvas, $18 \times 10$ inches
   Signed lower left: M J Heade
   Collection of Charles A. Sterling, Philadelphia, PA

36. *Orchids and Hummingbirds in a Tropical Landscape*
   Oil on canvas, $14^1/4 \times 22^1/8$ inches
   Signed lower right: M J Heade
   Collection of Charles A. Sterling, Philadelphia, PA

37. *Red Roses*
   Oil on canvas, $19 \times 11$ inches
   Signed lower right: M J Heade
   Collection of Charles A. Sterling, Philadelphia, PA

38. *Ruby Throat of North America*, 1865
   Oil on canvas, $11^3/4 \times 9^1/8$ inches
   Signed, dated, and inscribed on reverse: Ruby Throat
   United States M J Heade 1865
   Collection of Charles A. Sterling, Philadelphia, PA

HETZEL, George (1826-1899)

39. *Hanging Grouse*, 1876
   Oil on canvas mounted on masonite, $28 \times 17^1/2$ inches
   Signed and dated left side: Geo. Hetzel. 1876.
   Collection of Mr. and Mrs. Arthur C. Riley,
   Pittsburgh, PA

40. *Still Life*, 1865
    Oil on canvas, 15$^1/_2$ × 21$^1/_2$ inches
    Signed and dated lower left: Geo. Hetzel Sept. 1865
    Collection of Anthony P. Picadio, Pittsburgh, PA

41. *Still Life with Basket, Peaches, and White Grapes*, 1866
    Oil on canvas, 14$^1/_2$ × 20 inches
    Signed and dated lower right: Geo. Hetzel. 1866
    Collection of Westmoreland Museum of Art, Gift of the
    Women's Committee, Greensburg, PA

42. *Still Life with Concord Grapes and Apples*, ca. 1879
    Oil on canvas, 15$^1/_4$ × 24$^1/_4$ inches
    Signed lower right: Geo. Hetzel
    Collection of Westmoreland Museum of Art, William A.
    Coulter Fund, Greensburg, PA

43. *Still Life with Watermelon, Grapes, and Apples*, 1880
    Oil on canvas, 21$^7/_8$ × 20 inches
    Signed and dated lower left: Geo. Hetzel 1880
    Collection of Westmoreland Museum of Art, Mary
    Marchand Woods Memorial Fund, Greensburg, PA

44. *Still Life with Wild Game and Cat*, ca. 1855
    Oil on canvas, 28$^1/_4$ × 35$^3/_4$ inches
    Signed on reverse
    Collection of Westmoreland Museum of Art, Gift of
    Anthony P. Picadio, Greensburg, PA

45. *Two Dead Fowl*, 1878
    Oil on canvas, 20 × 29$^1/_2$ inches
    Signed and dated lower right: Geo. Hetzel 1878
    Private Collection

HETZEL, George T. (1846-1912)

46. *Hanging Grouse*, 1902
    Watercolor on paper, 21$^1/_2$ × 15$^1/_4$ inches
    Signed and dated lower left: G. Hetzel 1902
    Collection of Mr. and Mrs. Arthur C. Riley,
    Pittsburgh, PA

HETZEL, Lila B. (1873-1967)

47. *Grouse Hanging on a Door*, 1897
    Oil on canvas, 18$^1/_4$ × 12 inches
    Signed and dated lower left: L. B. Hetzel 97
    Collection of Westmoreland Museum of Art, Gift of
    Western Pennsylvania Conservancy, Pittsburgh, from
    the Dorothy Kantner Estate, in memory of George and
    Lila B. Hetzel, Greensburg, PA

HOBBS, George Thompson (1846-?)

48. *Stein and Pretzel*, 1886
    Oil on panel, 7$^1/_4$ × 9$^3/_4$ inches
    Signed and dated lower left: G T Hobbs 1886
    Collection of Kennedy Galleries, Inc., New York, NY

HOVENDEN, Thomas (1840-1895)

49. *Peonies*, 1886
    Oil on canvas, 20 × 24$^1/_8$ inches
    Signed with monogram lower left: TH; dated lower
    right: 1886
    Collection of The Pennsylvania Academy of the Fine
    Arts, Gift of Mrs. Edward H. Coates (The Edward H.
    Coates Memorial Collection), Philadelphia, PA

50. *Still Life with Fan and Roses*, 1874
    Oil on canvas, 9$^3/_8$ × 11$^1/_8$ inches
    Signed lower right: T Hovenden
    Collection of National Museum of American Art,
    Smithsonian Institution, Museum Purchase,
    Washington, DC

HOWELL, Edward A. (1848-1924)

51. *Brass Candle Stick*
    Oil on canvas, 12 × 17 inches
    Signed lower left: E. A. Howell
    Collection of The Reading Public Museum and Art
    Gallery, Reading, PA

KING, Albert F. (1854-1945)

52. *Hanging Hare*
    Oil on canvas, 27 × 16 inches
    Signed lower right: A F King
    Private Collection

53. *Late Night Snack*, ca. 1895
    Oil on canvas, 16 × 22$^1/_{16}$ inches
    Signed with initials lower right: AFK
    Collection of The Carnegie Museum of Art, Museum
    Purchase: Gift of R. K. Mellon Family Foundation, 1983,
    Pittsburgh, PA

54. *Pair of Grouse on Nature's Floor*, ca. 1930
    Oil on canvas, 20 × 32 inches
    Signed lower right: A. F. King
    Collection of Westmoreland Museum of Art, Director's
    Discretionary Fund, Greensburg, PA

55. *Still Life*, ca. 1900
    Oil on canvas, 12 × 18$^1/_4$ inches
    Signed lower right: A F King
    Collection of Mr. and Mrs. A. Dean Bartlett,
    Pittsburgh, PA

56. *Still Life*
    Oil on canvas, 17$^1/_2$ × 23$^1/_2$ inches
    Signed lower right: A. F. King
    Collection of Mr. and Mrs. Mario C. Celli,
    Greensburg, PA

57. *Still Life with Baskets, Grapes, and Apples*, ca. 1924
    Oil on canvas, 17$^5/_8$ × 24 inches
    Signed lower right: A.F. King
    Collection of Westmoreland Museum of Art, Gift of
    Frank E. Dowling, Greensburg, PA

58. *Still Life with Onions, Brown Jug, and Mackerel*
    Oil on canvas, 14 × 23 inches
    Signed lower right: A F King
    Westmoreland Museum of Art, Director's Discretionary
    Fund, Greensburg, PA

59. *Still Life with Strawberry Shortcake, Bottle of Chianti,
    Grapes, Oranges, and Wine Glass*, 1898
    Oil on canvas, 14 × 23 inches
    Signed and dated lower right: A. F. King 98
    Collection of Mr. and Mrs. Robert J. Salvatora,
    Gibsonia, PA

60. *Still Life with Watermelon, Cantaloupe, Grapes, and Apples*, ca. 1900
    Oil on canvas, 18 × 37 inches
    Signed lower right: A F King
    Westmoreland Museum of Art, William A. Coulter Fund, Greensburg, PA

61. *Woodcocks Hanging from a Nail*, ca. 1925
    Oil on canvas, 14 × 10 inches
    Signed lower right: A F King
    Collection of Westmoreland Museum of Art, Gift of Mr. and Mrs. Paul Sailer, Greensburg, PA

LAMBDIN, George Cochran (1830-1896)

62. *Autumn Sunshine*, 1880
    Oil on canvas, 30¹/₈ × 20 inches
    Signed and dated lower left: Geo. C. Lambdin 1880
    Collection of National Museum of American Art, Smithsonian Institution, Washington, DC

63. *In the Greenhouse*
    Oil on canvas, 31³/₁₆ × 40 inches
    Signed lower right: Geo. C. Lambdin
    Collection of The Metropolitan Museum of Art, Gift of Mrs. J. Augustus Barnard, 1979, New York, NY

64. *Roses and White Azaleas*
    Oil on panel, 24 × 11³/₄ inches
    Signed and dated lower right:
    Geo. C. Lambdin 1877
    Collection of Dr. and Mrs. Glenn H. Shepard, Newport News, VA

65. *Roses in a Chinese Vase*, ca. 1876
    Oil on canvas, 20 × 16 inches
    Signed lower right: Geo. C. Lambdin
    Collection of Lucille and Walter Rubin

66. *Roses in a Wheelbarrow*, ca. 1875
    Oil on canvas, 22¹/₄ × 30 inches
    Signed lower left: Geo. C. Lambdin
    Collection of R. H. Love Galleries, Inc., Chicago, IL

LANING, William M. (fl. 1850s)

67. *Still Life*, 1854
    Oil on canvas, 15¹/₂ × 19⁷/₈ inches
    Signed and dated lower left: Laning 1854
    Private Collection

LAWLER, Martin J. (Active 1870-1889)

68. *Trompe L'Oeil Still Life*, ca. 1889
    Oil on canvas board, 16 × 10 inches
    Signed on letter lower left: M. J. Lawler Erie, Pa.
    Collection of New York State Museum, Albany, NY

LEISSER, Martin B. (1846-1940)

69. *Design for the Franklin Literary Society Reunion*, Jan. 15, 1906
    Oil on board, 16¹/₂ × 12 inches
    Signed and dated lower left: M B. Leisser 1906
    Collection of Mr. and Mrs. Arthur C. Riley, Pittsburgh, PA

70. *Still Life with Watermelon*, 1890
    Oil on canvas, 17 × 26 inches
    Signed and dated lower left: M B Leisser 1890
    Collection of Mr. and Mrs. Robert J. Salvatora, Gibsonia, PA

LOGUE, John James (ca. 1810-after 1864)

71. *Still Life*
    Oil on canvas, 12 × 18 inches
    Signed, dated, and inscribed lower right
    Collection of Judy Johnson, M.D., Indianapolis, IN

McCLURG, Trevor (1816-1893)

72. *Still Life with Fruit and Silver Pitcher*, 1860
    Oil on canvas, 18¹/₂ × 15 inches
    Signed and dated lower left: Trevor McClurg 1860
    Collection of Mr. and Mrs. Arthur C. Riley, Pittsburgh, PA

MIFFLIN, Lloyd (1846-1921)

73. *Red Leaves and Berries*, 1873
    Oil on canvas, dia. 12 inches
    Signed and dated right side, lower third: Lloyd Mifflin 1873
    Collection of Franklin and Marshall College, College Collections, Lancaster, PA

NUNES, Abraham I. (fl. early 1800s)

74. *A Deception*, 1807
    Watercolor on paper, 24¹/₈ × 17⁷/₈ inches
    Signed, dated, and inscribed at center: BY A. I. NUNES, painted 1807; at lower left: A. I. Nunes fecit 1807; lower right: A. I. Nunes. dr(illeg.) pinxt. 1807
    Private Collection (Through the Courtesy of Philadelphia Museum of Art)

ORD, Joseph Biays (1805-1865)

75. *Still Life with Fruit and Game*, 1854
    Oil on canvas, 38 × 50 inches
    Signed and dated lower right: J. B. Ord. 1854
    Collection of Berry-Hill Galleries, New York, NY

PEALE, James (1749-1831)

76. *An Abundance of Fruit*, ca. 1820
    Oil on panel, 19¹/₄ × 26 inches
    Not signed, not dated
    Private Collection (Through the Courtesy of R. H. Love Galleries, Inc.)

77. *Fruit in a Chinese Export Basket*, 1822
    Oil on canvas, 16⁵/₈ × 21³/₄ inches
    Signed and dated on the basket's reserve: J Peale 1822
    Collection of Irwin Goldstein, M.D., Wayne, NJ

78. *Still Life with Grapes*
    Oil on canvas, 16 × 22 inches
    Not signed, not dated
    Collection of The Butler Institute of American Art, Youngstown, OH

79. *Still Life with Peaches and Grapes*, 1831
Oil on canvas, 14 × 19 inches
Signed and dated on reverse: Painted by James Peale in the 82nd year of his age, 1831
Collection of Mr. and Mrs. Donald D. Webster, Chevy Chase, MD

PEALE, Margaretta Angelica (1795-1882)

80. *Still Life: Grapes and Pomegranates*, 1820-29
Oil on canvas, 16¼ × 21⅛ inches
Signed and dated lower right: M A Peale 182
Collection of Maryland Historical Society, Gift of the Estate of J. Appleton Wilson through Miss Virginia A. Wilson, 1958, Baltimore, MD

81. *Strawberries and Cherries*
Oil on canvas, 10 × 12¼ inches
Not signed, not dated
Collection of the Pennsylvania Academy of the Fine Arts, Philadelphia, PA

PEALE, Mary Jane (1827-1902)

82. *Bouquet of Flowers*, 1858
Oil on panel, 15 × 12 inches
Signed lower right: M J Peale
Collection of Jerald Dillon Fessenden, New York, NY

83. *Still Life with Bowl of Fruit*, 1860
Oil on canvas, 19 × 27½ inches
Signed and dated on the reverse: 1860 at Riverside
Collection of Robert M. Poplack, Birmingham, MI

84. *Strawberries*
Oil on canvas, 9 × 13¼
Not signed, not dated
Private Collection

PEALE, Raphaelle (1774-1825)

85. *Still Life with Raisins, Yellow and Red Apples in Porcelain Basket*, ca. 1820-22
Oil on wood, 12¾ × 19 inches
Signed lower right: Raphaelle Peale
Gift of Mrs. Francis White, from the Collection of Mrs. Miles White, Jr., Baltimore, MD

86. *Still Life with Raisin Cake*, 1813
Oil on panel, 11½ × 8½ inches
Signed and dated lower right: Raphaelle Peale 1813
Private Collection

PEALE, Rubens (1784-1865)

87. *Still Life*, 1857
Oil on canvas, 19 × 27 inches
Signed and dated on the reverse: Painted by Rubens Peale 1857
Collection of Kennedy Galleries, Inc., New York, NY

88. *Watermelon Slice with Peaches and Grapes*, 1863
Oil on canvas, 18½ × 27¼ inches
Signed lower right: Rubens Peale; signed and dated on reverse: Rubens Peale Aged 79 1863
Collection of the Westmoreland Museum of Art, Anonymous Donor, by Exchange, Greensburg, PA

PEALE, Titian Ramsay (1799-1885)

89. *Still Life with Flowers and Insects*, 1879
Watercolor, 9½ × 8⅜ inches
Signed and dated lower right: Titian Ramsay Peale 1879
Collection of Westmoreland Museum of Art, Mary Marchand Woods Memorial Fund, Greensburg, PA

PETO, John Frederick (1854-1907)

90. *Artist Palette with Beer Mug and Pipe*
Oil on wood panel, 13½ × 9 inches
Not signed, not dated
Collection of Kennedy Galleries, Inc., New York, NY

91. *Books on a Table*, ca. 1900
Oil on canvas, 24½ × 43 inches
Not signed, not dated
Collection of James Maroney, Inc., New York, NY

92. *Crumbs of Comfort*, 1881
Oil on canvas, 12 × 15 inches
Signed and dated lower right: J. F. Peto 11.81
Collection of Robert M. Poplack, Birmingham, MI

93. *Homage au Chardin*
Oil on canvas, 22 × 30 inches
Not signed, not dated
Collection of James and Faith Stewart-Gordon, New York, NY

94. *Lantern and Bowie Knife*, ca. 1887
Oil on canvas, 20¼ × 10¼ inches
Signed lower left: J F Peto
Collection of Kennedy Galleries, Inc., New York, NY

95. *Lincoln and the $25 Note*, 1904
Oil on canvas, 20⅛ × 14⅛ inches
Signed lower left: John F Peto
Collection of Jean and Alvin Snowiss, Lock Haven, PA

96. *Rack Picture for William Malcolm Bunn*, 1882
Oil on canvas, 24 × 20 inches
Signed and dated lower right: J. F. Peto 82
Collection of National Museum of American Art, Smithsonian Institution, Gift of Nathaly Baum in Memory of Harry Baum, Washington, DC

97. *Ten Dollar Bill*
Oil on canvas, 17 × 21 inches
Signed lower left: J. P.
Private Collection

PIPPIN, Horace (1888-1946)

98. *Potted Plant in the Window*
Oil on canvas, 7 × 9 inches
Not signed, not dated
Collection of Brandywine River Museum, Chadds Ford, PA

RAMSEY, Milne (1846-1915)

99. *Still Life*, 1869
Oil on canvas, 12⅛ × 16 inches
Signed lower right of center: Ramsey
Private Collection

100. *Still Life: Pistols and Blue Vase*, 1911
Oil on canvas, 22 × 30 inches
Signed and dated lower left: Milne Ramsey II
Private Collection

READIO, Wilfred A. (1895-1961)

101. *Curtained Window*, 1926
Oil on canvas, 30 × 36 inches
Signed and dated lower right: Wilfred Allen Readio 1926
Collection of The Board of Public Education,
Pittsburgh, PA

ROESEN, Severin (active 1848-1871)

102. *Still Life Bouquet*, ca. 1867
Oil on canvas, 50 × 36 inches
Signed lower right on drapery: S. Roesen
Private Collection

103. *Still Life with Fruit*
Oil on canvas, 36 × 50 inches
Signed lower right: Roesen
Collection of Westmoreland Museum of Art, William A.
Coulter Fund, Greensburg, PA

SHEELER, Charles (1883-1965)

104. *Cactus*, 1931
Oil on canvas, 45 × 30 inches
Signed and dated lower right: Sheeler 1931
Collection of Philadelphia Museum of Art, Louise and
Walter Arensberg Collection, Philadelphia, PA

STREET, Robert (1796-1865)

105. *The Basket of Apples*, 1818
Oil on board, 10 × 14 1/8 inches
Signed and dated lower right: Street 1818
Collection of Flint Institute of Arts, Gift of the Viola E.
Bray Charitable Trust, Flint, MI

TAYLOR, Charles Jay (1885-1929)

106. *Still Life*
Oil on canvas, 16 × 20 inches
Signed lower right: C. J. Taylor
Collection of Westmoreland Museum of Art, Gift of Mrs.
Beatrice Nash Marshall, Greensburg, PA

TORREY, Hiram Dwight (1820-1900)

107. *Still Life with Flowers and Fruit*, 1865
Oil on panel, 23 × 19 1/2 inches
Signed and dated lower right: H D Torrey Pinxt 1865
Collection of Mr. and Mrs. John G. Black, Warrior
Marks, PA

TOWNE, Rosalba (Rosa) M. (1827-1909)

108. *Wildflowers, Leaves, and Berries*, 1827
Watercolor, 12 × 9 1/2 inches
Signed lower left: R Towne
Collection of Westmoreland Museum of Art, Gift of Mrs.
Donald Thompson, Jr. and Mrs. Aiken W. Fisher,
Greensburg, PA

WOOD, Jr., George Bacon (1832-1910)

109. *Leaf and Berry Study*, 1864
Oil on paper, 7 1/4 × 6 3/4 inches
Signed and dated lower right: G. B. Wood, Jr. Philad.
1864
Collection of Mr. and Mrs. Wilbur L. Ross, Jr., New
York, NY

110. *Study from Nature*, ca. 1866
Oil on canvas, 10 1/4 × 15 inches
Signed lower left: Geo B Wood Jr
Collection of Mr. and Mrs. William G. Coughlin,
Brookline, MA

WOODSIDE, Sr., John Archibald (1781-1852)

111. *Still Life: Rabbits*, 1821
Oil on paper on canvas, 23 1/4 × 18 3/4 inches
Signed and dated lower right: J. A. Woodside 1821
Collection of Philadelphia Museum of Art, Bequest of
Robert Nebinger, Philadelphia, PA

WOOSTER, Austin C. (active 1864-1913)

112. *Hanging Grapes*, 1892
Oil on canvas, 28 1/4 × 12 inches
Signed and dated lower right: A. C. Wooster 1892;
Inscribed: Painted by Austin C. Wooster and dated 1892
on the reverse
Collection of The Cooley Gallery, Inc., Old Lyme, CT

113. *Still Life with Apples*, 1907
Oil on canvas, 16 1/4 × 20 inches
Signed and dated lower right: A. C. Wooster 07
Collection of Mr. and Mrs. A. Dean Bartlett,
Pittsburgh, PA

114. *Still Life with Grapes and Oranges*, 1899
Oil on canvas, 7 1/2 × 11 1/2 inches
Signed and dated lower right: ACW 99; signed and
dated on reverse by Austin C. Wooster 1899
Collection of Dr. and Mrs. Howard M. Tanning,
Pittsburgh, PA

115. *Straw Hat with Peaches*, 1897
Oil on canvas, 16 × 22 inches
Signed and dated lower right: A. C. Wooster 1897;
Signed on the reverse: Austin. C. Wooster – 1896 –
Collection of Westmoreland Museum of Art, Gift of Mrs.
Constance B. Mellon, by Exchange, Greensburg, PA

WYETH, Newell Convers (1882-1945)

116. *Still Life with Iris and Oranges*
Oil on canvas, 36 × 40 inches
Signed lower right: To my friend Bill Phelps from NCW
Collection of Delaware Art Museum, Gift of Mary M. R.
Phelps, Wilmington, DE

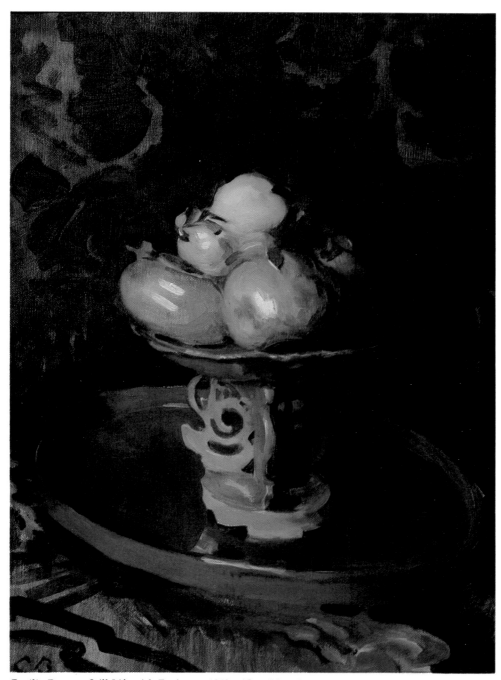

Cecilia Beaux, *Still Life with Fruit,* ca. 1918 (Cat. No. 6)

Hugh Henry Breckenridge, *The Flower Garden,* ca. 1906  (Cat. No. 11)

Fidelia Bridges, *Still Life with Robin's Nest*, 1863   (Cat. No. 12)

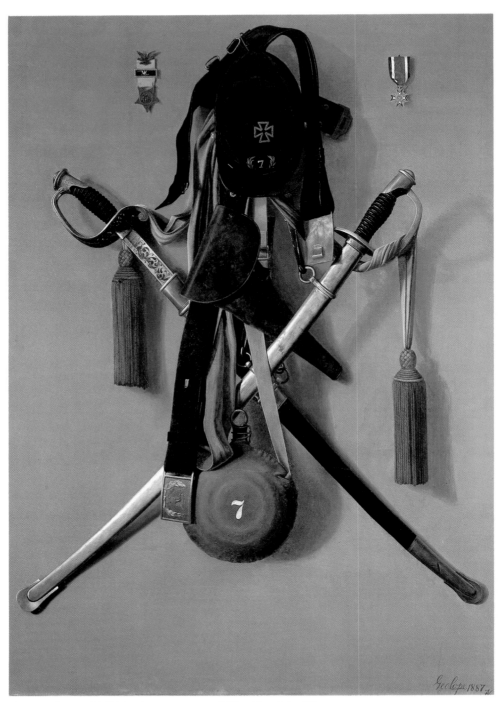

George Cope, *Civil War Accoutrements*, 1887   (Cat. No. 13)

Charles Demuth, *Zinnia Bouquet*, 1925   (Cat. No. 20)

William Michael Harnett, *After the Hunt (3rd Version)*, 1884   (Cat. No. 29)

John F. Francis, *An Abundance of Fruit*   (Cat. No. 23)

John F. Francis, *Fruit and Wine,* 1858   (Cat. No. 24)

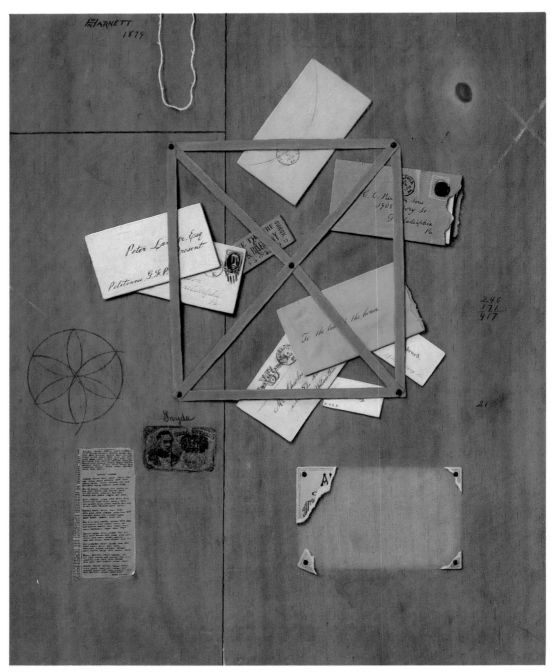

William Michael Harnett, *The Artist's Letter Rack,* 1879   (Cat. No. 30)

William Michael Harnett, *Philadelphia Public Ledger,* 1880   (Cat. No. 31)

Martin Johnson Heade, *Orchids and Hummingbirds in a Tropical Landscape*   (Cat. No. 36)

Martin Johnson Heade, *Cherokee Roses in a Glass*  (Cat. No. 35)

Martin Johnson Heade, *Red Roses*   (Cat. No. 37)

Martin Johnson Heade, *Ruby Throat of North America*, 1865  (Cat. No. 38)

18

George Hetzel, *Still Life with Watermelon, Grapes, and Apples*, 1880  (Cat. No. 43)

George Cochran Lambdin, *Roses in a Wheelbarrow*, ca. 1875  (Cat. No. 66)

Albert F. King, *Still Life with Watermelon, Cantaloupe, Grapes, and Apples,* ca. 1900 (Cat. No. 60)

Joseph Biays Ord, *Still Life with Fruit and Game,* 1854 (Cat. No. 75)

George Cochran Lambdin, *In the Greenhouse*   (Cat. No. 63)

James Peale, *An Abundance of Fruit,* ca. 1820  (Cat. No. 76)

Raphaelle Peale, *Still Life with Raisin Cake,* 1813  (Cat. No. 86)

22

Rubens Peale, *Watermelon Slice with Peaches and Grapes,* 1863   (Cat. No. 88)

Severin Roesen, *Still Life with Fruit*   (Cat. No. 103)

23

John Frederick Peto, *Lantern and Bowie Knife,* ca. 1887   (Cat. No. 94)

John Frederick Peto, *Lincoln and the $25 Note*, 1904   (Cat. No. 95)

John Frederick Peto, *Ten Dollar Bill*   (Cat. No. 97)

26

Severin Roesen, *Still Life Bouquet,* ca. 1867   (Cat. No. 102)

Jacob Atkinson, *Souvenir of the Columbian Exposition*, 1893 (Cat. No. 1)

Henry Kepple Beck, *Still Life* (Cat. No. 7)

Ben Austrian, *Hanging Game (Two Ducks),* 1909   (Cat. No. 2)

Ben Austrian, *Hanging Game (Three Ducks)*, 1909   (Cat. No. 3)

Ben Austrian, *The Paper Rack*   (Cat. No. 4)

Andre Avinoff, *Dutch Floral Arrangement*   (Cat. No. 5)

Thomas Birch, *Still Life*   (Cat. No. 8)

David Gilmour Blythe, *Old Age,* 1865   (Cat. No. 9)

David Gilmour Blythe, *Youth,* 1865  (Cat. No. 10)

Fred A. Demmler, *Still Life with Violin,* ca. 1909  (Cat. No. 16)

34

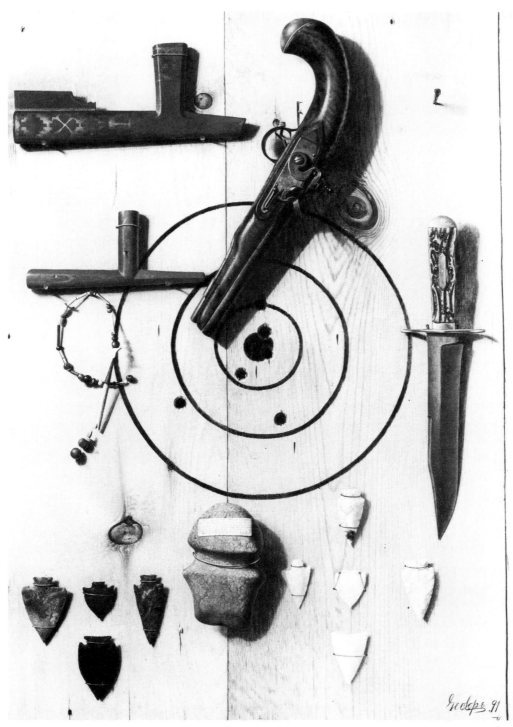

George Cope, *Indian Relics,* 1891   (Cat. No. 14)

Fred A. Demmler, *Still Life with Pineapple*   (Cat. No. 15)

36

Charles Demuth, *Cyclamen*, 1905   (Cat. No. 17)

Charles Demuth, *Daffodils*, 1928   (Cat. No. 18)

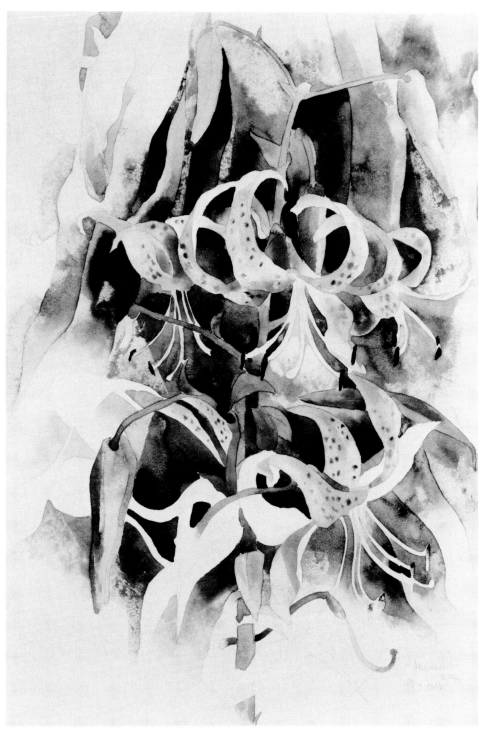

Charles Demuth, *Tiger Lilies*, 1920   (Cat. No. 19)

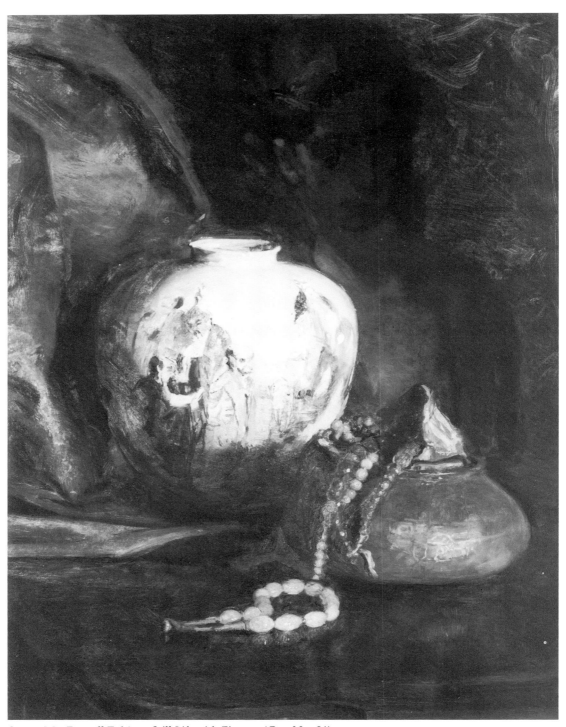

Susan MacDowell Eakins, *Still Life with Figure* (Cat. No. 21)

Emil Foerster, *Still Life with Peach, Grapes, and Plum,* 1863   (Cat. No. 22)

John F. Francis, *Still Life: A Luncheon Table,* 1852   (Cat. No. 25)

William Glackens, *Still Life with Three Glasses*   (Cat. No. 26)

Aaron Henry Gorson, *Still Life: Two Oranges*   (Cat. No. 27)

Johanna Knowles Woodwell Hailman, *Flowers,* ca. 1920   (Cat. No. 28)

William Michael Harnett, *Shinplaster with Exhibition Label and Newspaper Clipping,*
1879   (Cat. No. 32)

William Michael Harnett, *Still Life,* 1875   (Cat. No. 33)

William Michael Harnett, *Still Life with a Letter to Mr. Lask,* 1879   (Cat. No. 34)

44

George Hetzel, *Hanging Grouse*, 1876 (Cat. No. 39)

George Hetzel, *Still Life*, 1865 (Cat. No. 40)

George Hetzel, *Still Life with Basket, Peaches, and White Grapes*, 1866 (Cat. No. 41)

George Hetzel, *Still Life with Concord Grapes and Apples*, 1879 (Cat. No. 42)

George Hetzel, *Still Life with Wild Game and Cat*, ca. 1855 (Cat. No. 44)

47

George Hetzel, *Two Dead Fowl*, 1878   (Cat. No. 45)

George Thompson Hobbs, *Stein and Pretzel*, 1886   (Cat. No. 48)

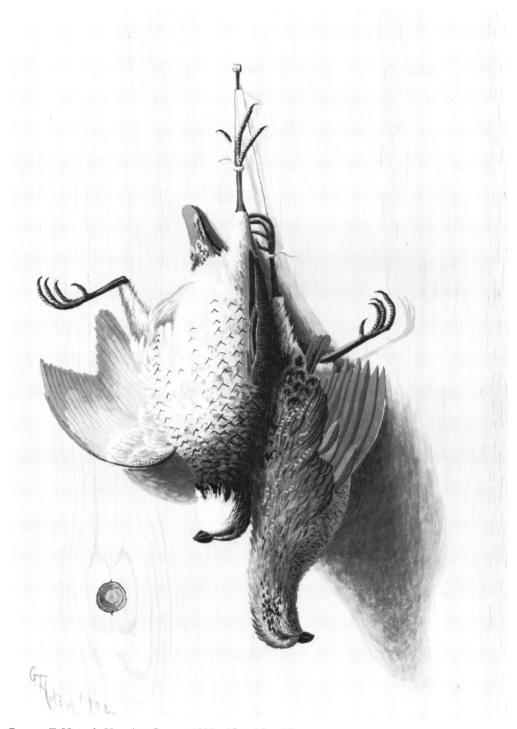

George T. Hetzel, *Hanging Grouse,* 1902   (Cat. No. 46)

Lila B. Hetzel, *Grouse Hanging on a Door,* 1897   (Cat. No. 47)

Thomas Hovenden, *Peonies,* 1886   (Cat. No. 49)

Thomas Hovenden, *Still Life with Fan and Roses,* 1874   (Cat. No. 50)

Edward A. Howell, *Brass Candle Stick* (Cat. No. 51)

Albert F. King, *Late Night Snack,* ca. 1895 (Cat. No. 53)

Albert F. King, *Hanging Hare* (Cat. No. 52)

Albert F. King, *Pair of Grouse on Nature's Floor,* ca. 1930   (Cat. No. 54)

Albert F. King, *Still Life,* ca. 1900   (Cat. No. 55)

Albert F. King, *Still Life*   (Cat. No. 56)

Albert F. King, *Still Life with Baskets, Grapes, and Apples,* ca. 1924   (Cat. No. 57)

Albert F. King, *Still Life with Onions, Brown Jug, and Mackeral* (Cat. No. 58)

Albert F. King, *Still Life with Strawberry Shortcake, Bottle of Chianti, Grapes, Oranges, and Wine Glass,* 1898 (Cat. No. 59)

56

Albert F. King, *Woodcocks Hanging from a Nail*, ca. 1925   (Cat. No. 61)

George Cochran Lambdin, *Autumn Sunshine*, 1880 (Cat. No. 62)

George Cochran Lambdin, *Roses and White Azaleas*   (Cat. No. 64)

George Cochran Lambdin, *Roses in a Chinese Vase,* ca. 1876 (Cat. No. 65)

William M. Laning, *Still Life*, 1854   (Cat. No. 67)

Martin B. Leisser, *Still Life with Watermelon*, 1890   (Cat. No. 70)

61

Martin J. Lawler, *Trompe L'Oeil Still Life*, ca. 1889  (Cat. No. 68)

Martin B. Leisser, *Design for the Franklin Literary Society Reunion*, Jan. 15, 1906   (Cat. No. 69)

John James Logue, *Still Life*   (Cat. No. 71)

James Peale, *Fruit in a Chinese Export Basket*, 1822   (Cat. No. 77)

64

Trevor McClurg, *Still Life with Fruit and Silver Pitcher,* 1860   (Cat. No. 72)

Lloyd Mifflin, *Red Leaves and Berries,* 1873 (Cat. No. 73)

66

Abraham I. Nunes, *A Deception,* 1807   (Cat. No. 74)

James Peale, *Still Life with Grapes*   (Cat. No. 78)

James Peale, *Still Life with Peaches and Grapes*, 1831   (Cat. No. 79)

Margaretta Angelica Peale, *Still Life: Grapes and Pomegranates,* 1820-29   (Cat. No. 80)

Margaretta Angelica Peale, *Strawberries and Cherries*   (Cat. No. 81)

Mary Jane Peale, *Bouquet of Flowers,* 1858  (Cat. No. 82)

Mary Jane Peale, *Still Life with Bowl of Fruit,* 1860 (Cat. No. 83)

Mary Jane Peale, *Strawberries* (Cat. No. 84)

Raphaelle Peale, *Still Life with Raisins, Yellow and Red Apples in Porcelain Basket,* ca. 1820-22
(Cat. No. 85)

Rubens Peale, *Still Life,* 1857   (Cat. No. 87)

Titian Ramsay Peale, *Still Life with Flowers and Insects*, 1879   (Cat. No. 89)

John Frederick Peto, *Artist Palette with Beer Mug and Pipe*   (Cat. No. 90)

74

John Frederick Peto, *Books on a Table,* ca. 1900   (Cat. No. 91)

John Frederick Peto, *Crumbs of Comfort,* 1881   (Cat. No. 92)

John Frederick Peto, *Homage au Chardin*   (Cat. No. 93)

Horace Pippin, *Potted Plant in the Window*   (Cat. No. 98)

John Frederick Peto, *Rack Picture for William Malcolm Bunn*, 1882 (Cat. No. 96)

Milne Ramsey, *Still Life: Pistols and Blue Vase*, 1911    (Cat. No. 100)

Milne Ramsey, *Still Life*, 1869    (Cat. No. 99)

Wilfred A. Readio, *Curtained Window,* 1926   (Cat. No. 101)

Robert Street, *The Basket of Apples,* 1818   (Cat. No. 105)

Charles Sheeler, *Cactus,* 1931   (Cat. No. 104)

Charles Jay Taylor, *Still Life*   (Cat. No. 106)

George Bacon Wood, Jr., *Study from Nature*, ca. 1866   (Cat. No. 110)

Hiram Dwight Torrey, *Still Life with Flowers and Fruit,* 1865   (Cat. No. 107)

Rosalba (Rosa) M. Towne, *Wildflowers, Leaves, and Berries*, 1827   (Cat. No. 108)

George Bacon Wood, Jr., *Leaf and Berry Study,* 1864   (Cat. No. 109)

84

John Archibald Woodside, Sr., *Still Life: Rabbits,* 1821   (Cat. No. 111)

Austin C. Wooster, *Hanging Grapes,* 1892   (Cat. No. 112)

Austin C. Wooster, *Still Life with Apples,* 1907 (Cat. No. 113)

Austin C. Wooster, *Still Life with Grapes and Oranges,* 1899 (Cat. No. 114)

Austin C. Wooster, *Straw Hat with Peaches*, 1897   (Cat. No. 115)

Newell Convers Wyeth, *Still Life with Iris and Oranges*   (Cat. No. 116)

# DICTIONARY OF ARTISTS

This list of artists is provided as a historical record of still life painters working and exhibiting in Pennsylvania from 1795 through the 1930s. For this information we researched the exhibition records of the Pennsylvania Academy of the Fine Arts in Philadelphia; *American Still-Life Painting* by William H. Gerdts and Russell Burke was thoroughly consulted for additional information. The Westmoreland Museum of Art's catalogue, *Southwestern Pennsylvania Painters, 1800-1945*, provided a group of artists new to the artistic literature of this state. Biographies for most of the artists are included. Our research turned up a number of artists who remain obscure except for an exhibition entry and date; however, they have also been included. It is frustrating that records are not available for some artists' birth and death dates, or where they were born or the city in which they died. And as a final point of information concerning our list of artists, biographies of major artists such as Harnett, Peto or Sheeler, just to mention a few, were kept brief knowing that major monographs on these artists are in print.

*The following abbreviations and their identifications are used throughout the biographies:*

| | |
|---|---|
| AFS | The Artists Fund Society |
| HRPAD | *History of the Rise and Progress of Design in America* by William Dunlap |
| MMA | Metropolitan Museum of Art |
| NAD | National Academy of Design |
| NYHS | New York Historical Society |
| PAFA | Pennsylvania Academy of the Fine Arts |
| QV | See also |
| SAA | Society of American Artists |
| T-B | Thieme-Becker |
| WHG | William H. Gerdts |

## ALDEN, Mrs.

Exhibited in 1832, at the annual of the PAFA, a painting *The Dutch Kitchen*, a copy after an unnamed artist.

## ALLBRIGHT, William (ca. 1795-?)

Allbright lived in Philadelphia where he served as a drawing master. Little of his work is known, however, his drawings on stone for *The Floral Magazine and Botanical Repositor* published 1832-1834 by D. & C. Landreth Nursery and Seedsmen was among the earliest magazines published by lithography in America. The magazine's primary purpose was to make the public aware of the variety of seeds available from the magazine's publisher. It did, however, serve to popularize some flowers, e.g., Camillia japonica. The magazine followed the lead of English botanical periodical which tended to be more scientific in nature.

## ANCKER, Adolphe

Thought to have been a pupil of J. F. Peto's in Island Heights, New Jersey. Two small paintings attributed to this artist were on the New York art market, ca. 1985. If Ancker was in fact a pupil of Peto's, he would be one of the few known, despite the artist's business card stating that he gave "Instructions in painting." Peto added, however, that "terms" would have to be in advance.

## ANCORA, Pietro

A drawing master as well as a painter of religious and still life paintings, Ancora was the proprietor of an art gallery in Philadelphia. Arriving from Italy around 1800, Ancora was associated with Bell & Ancora's art gallery in 1819. Among his American pupils were John Neagle and D. H. Strother. Strother was known as the artist "Porte Crayon," and he exhibited at the Pennsylvania Academy and the Artist's Fund Society from 1829-1843. T-B notes that Ancora was in Naples in 1805, but he is listed in the Philadelphia city directories for that year.

## ARNOLD, Victor

(1863, 772 Moss St.; 1864, 5 S. 6th St.; 1865, 772 Moss St., Philadelphia)

Exhibited in the PAFA 1863, 1864, 1865 paintings of *Fruit* listed in the catalogue as "for sale."

## ATKINSON, Jacob (1864-1938)

Painter in the trompe l'oeil tradition, said to have been a letter carrier in Philadelphia who painted still lifes of mail and money to amuse himself. The artist, perhaps in a veiled reference to time, served as a Civil War soldier. In the post-war period, postal service jobs were often given as patronage to veterans. The envelope includes a remark of a soldier's tent emblazoned "OUR COUNTRY" beneath a waving Union flag. Also included are a Ten Dollar Treasury note of the 1891 series and the ubiquitous Ten-Cent "shinplaster" found in so many artists of this school's work. He has addressed the letter to a Benjamin Atkinson, Sarjent Street, Philadelphia. The painting included in our exhibition, *Souvenir of the Columbian Exposition*, is replete with references to the Columbian World's Exposition of 1893, the year this painting was created. An envelope addressed to "Mr. John Smith Philada Pa." is stamped "Due 1¢" and bearing the commemorative stamp of "Columbus in Sight of Land" (one cent) mailed from Kensington Station, Philadelphia. This is pasted over an embossed commemorative Columbian envelope which bear the stamp "Columbia Station Oct 4 2 PM Philadelphia," perhaps a first day of issue. Beneath these are two postcards: an "Official Souvenir Postal" of the fair and posted from "World's Fair Station October 24." The artist seems to have taken an above average interest in matters philatelic. There is also another of the Columbian stamp affixed to a trompe l'oeil wood grain support of the 4-cent "Fleet of Columbus."

AUSTRIAN, Ben (1870-1921)
(1252 Perkiomen St., Reading, PA)
Born in Reading, Pa., he worked briefly as a salesman in Williamsport, Pa., after which he returned to Reading. He became famous as a painter of chickens and is perhaps best known for a baby chick in the trademark for Bon Ami cleanser. He died in Palm Beach, Fla.

AVINOFF, Andre (1884-1949)
Andre Avinoff was born in the Ukraine to one of Russia's most distinguished families. As a young man, he studied law and several years later became assistant secretary-general of the Senate in Saint Petersburg. At age 27, he was made gentleman-in-waiting to Czar Nicholas II.

Avinoff first came to America during early World War I to buy supplies for the all-Russian Zemsky Union (similar to the American Red Cross). When the Communist Revolution occurred in 1917, he fled Russia and returned to the United States, leaving behind his prized collection of 80,000 Asian and Arctic butterflies. This valuable collection, which includes specimens named for Avinoff, is housed today in the Academy of Science in Leningrad. It is considered one of the most complete butterfly collections in the world.

Avinoff's entomologist's skills next brought him to Pittsburgh when Carnegie Museum invited him to catalog its butterfly collection. In 1926, upon the death of Dr. Douglas Stewart, the directorship went to Dr. Avinoff. The new director could speak four languages and read ten. One of his innovations was to exhibit animals in replicas of natural habitats rather than unadorned cases.

It is difficult to imagine a life fuller than Avinoff's. Aside from his careers as entomologist and museum director, he was also a dedicated artist who worked in a variety of styles. It has been said that "he makes the real approach the symbolic, without losing exact description." He painted dream and memory paintings; he created opulent Persian portraits, Jamaican pictures, and gentle landscapes. His "Lost Atlantis" employs the symbolism of Russian myth.

Perhaps the most important artistic contribution was his watercolors of flowers, which appeared in *Wildflowers of Western Pennsylvania*. The two-volume set was published in 1953 to a burst of critical acclaim.

Following his retirement in 1945, Avinoff lived in Locust Valley, L.I., with his sister Mme. Elizabeth Shoumatoff, the artist who was sketching a portrait of Franklin D. Roosevelt when the president suffered his fatal stroke in his Warm Springs cottage.

BABB, Harriet Trevette
(1334 Chestnut St., Philadelphia)
Exh. PAFA, 1886 *Chrysanthemums* cat. no. 3

90

BAILLY, Joseph Alexis (1825-1883)
Exhibited three-dimensional still lifes. Bailly was a friend of the Woodside family and in 1853 he carved a memorial to Abraham Woodside, which included a bust of the deceased.

BALCH, Edwin S.
(1520 Chestnut St., Philadelphia)
Exh. PAFA, 1886 *A Study of Flowers* cat. no. 8
He was born in Philadelphia and was a pupil of Henri Marcette and Thomas Eakins.

BARBER, Alice
(639 N. 12th St., Philadelphia)
Exh. PAFA, 1886 *Yellow Iris* cat. no. 10

BARNES, Penelope Birch (active 1812-1840)
An active contributor to the annual exhibitions of the PAFA, SAA, and AFS. In 1813 and 1814, she was living with her father, the artist William Birch at his home Springland near Bristol, Pa; from 1829 on she was living in Philadelphia.

BARTON, Benjamin Smith (1776-1815)
Artist-naturalist. Friend of Alexander Wilson, William Bartream, and Charles Willson Peale. Succeeded Benjamin Rush as professor of medicine at the University of Pennsylvania. Born in Lancaster, PA, the son of an Episcopalian minister, who was a naturalist himself. Studied at the College of Philadelphia and in Europe. Early in his career he is known to have made floral drawings and landscapes. While nothing is known of his training as a draftsman, the extremely high quality of those drawings that survive suggest that he may have had further training, perhaps in conjunction with his medical or scientific studies abroad.

BATES, Dewey (1851-?)
City directories list him in Philadelphia until 1899. Bates enrolled in Gerome's atelier in September 1874. After his studies in Paris, he returned to Philadelphia where he lived at 607 North 7th Street (1869). That year he exhibited *An Ivy Study*, which he listed for sale. This must have been related to the studies of ferns and ivy that were popular productions from the brush of William Trost Richards.

BEACH, Martha Edwards
(1416 Chestnut, Philadelphia)
Exh. PAFA, 1889 *Mermet Roses* cat. no. 11
Born in Connecticut, she studied at PAFA and with Milne Ramsey.

BEAUX, Cecelia (1855-1942)
Beaux was born in Philadelphia, PA in 1855 and died in Gloucester, MA in 1942. Raised by two aunts and her ma-

ternal grandmother, Beaux was taught at an early age the value of a job well done, dedication, and the joy of creation. Until age 14 she had no education outside the home. Her first art training was with Katherine Drinker, a distant relative, later augmented by classes with Dutch artist Adolf Van der Whelen and with William Sartain from whom she learned the dark palette of Munich school painting. A portrait of her sister and nephew of 1883-85 was her first major canvas and was accepted at the Paris Salon in 1887. The following year she left for Paris herself and entered the Julian Academy for instruction from Bougereau and Fleury. This experience lightened her palette and loosened her brushwork but she never adopted the light-dissolved forms of the Impressionists.

She took a studio in New York in 1890 and after a brief period of re-adjustment, began producing portraits of highly original composition executed with sensitive and confident technique. Color and texture became important elements in her work arranged for surface effect as well as to heighten expressiveness.

Her career well established, she made a brief trip abroad in 1896 and met Monet, whose work she admired, at Giverny. A series of double, full-length portraits begun in 1898 have the fluidity of handling of John Singer Sargent. Bold fabric patterns are masterfully incorporated into her compositions for increased contrast, vitality and texture. Praised for putting "brains into her work," the surface qualities of her painting reinforce the inner relationships suggested by her compositions. Her portraits often included still life elements but the small *Still Life* in the WMA collection is her only known isolated example of this theme and may have been conceived as a study. (However, the *New York American* of January 14, 1918, mentions a Beaux still life being exhibited at Arden Gallery in 1918.) It is painted with the same freedom of brushwork and dynamic use of color, texture and pattern as in her portraits.

Beaux remained active and enthusiastic about her work throughout her life despite failing health. In 1919 she went to Europe to paint three portraits for the U. S. War Portraits Commission and was the first American woman commissioned by the Italian Ministry of Public Instruction to do a self-portrait for the Uffizi Gallery, Florence. Her autobiography, *Background With Figures*, was published in 1930. In addition to frequent guest lectures, she taught at the Pennsylvania Academy of Fine Arts 1895 to 1916, the first, full-time, female faculty member.

BECK, Henry Kepple (1862-1937)
Born in Harrisburg, Pa. and died in Harrisburg, Pa.

Beck painted portraits and landscapes. After studying with his artist father, he traveled in 1889 to Munich and to Italy. He then went to Paris where he studied with Blanc, Curtois, and Gerome. When he returned to Harrisburg, he became active with a sketch group which later became the Harrisburg Art Association and was a founding member.

BECK, J. Augustus (1831-after 1912)
Sculptor, portrait and landscape artist. Born in Lititz, PA. In 1831 he studied with Thomas Crawford and Hiram Powers in Italy. Living in Philadelphia in 1856 and Lancaster in 1858, he settled in Harrisburg in 1861 where he would spend the rest of his life. A large collection of copies of his portraits is in the Philadelphia Historical Society. Beck exhibited a single still life at the PAFA in 1866.

BECK, Robert K.
   (729 Walnut St., Philadelphia)
   Exh. PAFA, 1885 *Still Life* cat. no. 21
Born in 1862, Pottsville, PA, Beck studied at PAFA, Penna. Museum School of Industrial Art, and Art Students' League, N.Y.

BIRCH, William (1755-1834)
One still life attributed to him is illustrated in WHG Birch exhibition catalogue. Birch is known to have exhibited a still life at the AFS in 1837.

BIRCH, Thomas (1779-1851)
Thomas Birch was born in England and was brought to Philadelphia in 1794 by his father, William Birch, who trained him as a painter and engraver. The War of 1812 inspired him to paint a series of naval engagements which made his fame. His marine and winter scenes are particularly attractive. Father and son worked together on the famous "Views of Philadelphia," which were published in 1800.

BITTNER, Frank
   Exh. PAFA, 1908 *Still Life* cat. no. 127

BLOCH, Julius T. (1888-?)
   Exh. PAFA, 1916 *Asters* cat. no. 245 and *Lilacs* cat. no. 339; 1921 *Marigolds* cat. no. 289, *The Old Leeds Chocolate Pot* cat. no. 319, and *Chrysanthemums* cat. no. 413; 1922 *A Basket of Fruit* cat. no. 322; 1927 *Tulips and Anemones* cat. no. 296; 1928 *Cosmos and Zinnias* cat. no. 220, and *Field Flowers* cat. no. 264; 1929 *Mid-Summer Flowers* cat. no. 126, and *A Bouquet* cat. no. 177

BLYTHE, David Gilmour (1815-1865)
Born in East Liverpool, Ohio and died in Pittsburgh, Pa. Blythe demonstrated artistic talent early in life and at age 16 was apprenticed to Joseph Woodwell, a Pittsburgh woodcarver. He travelled down the Mississippi River with his brother and to Boston, New York, Florida and the West Indies with the Navy before returning to East Liverpool to work as an itinerant portrait painter. Around 1846 he moved to Uniontown, Pennsylvania where he was commissioned to carve a nine-foot statue of General

Lafayette for the dome of the county courthouse. Prone to depression since childhood, Blythe's attitude became increasingly restless and eccentric after the death of his very young wife and his cynicism surfaces in the caustic sentiment of some of his genre scenes. He toured the western Pennsylvania-Ohio area with his painted, 300-foot panorama that wound on rollers to display one scene at a time. Eventually he returned to East Liverpool to paint portraits again and spent the last decade of his life in Pittsburgh.

Blythe's work was influenced by his travels and most importantly by the communities in which he worked and lived. Essentially self-taught, Blythe worked in a highly accomplished, realistic style with composition, color and modeling adjusted to each subject. His unusual insight into human nature and its foibles sparked his natural gift for pictorial conception. The results are vividly mirrored images of the colorful, cosmopolitan life of 19th century Pittsburgh.

BORDLEY, John Beale (1800-1882)

BRAID, Christina F.
> (2238 Ridge Ave., Philadelphia)
> Exh. PAFA, 1885 *Apples* cat. no. 38; 1886 *Study in Still Life* cat. no. 27; 1891 *Fruit* cat. no. 22

Born in Scotland, she studied in Philadelphia School of Design for Women and under George C. Lambdin. She also studied with Carl Weber.

BRANSON, Isabel Cartwright
> Exh. PAFA, 1921 *Summer Flowers* cat. no. 320

BRECKENRIDGE, Hugh H. (1870-?)
> Exh. PAFA, 1915 *Old China* cat. no. 385, *The Chinese Jar* cat. no. 387, and *Peonies* cat. no. 434; 1916 *Eggplants* cat. no. 261 and *Ivory, Gold, and Blue* cat. no. 295; 1917 various still lifes cat. no. 321-333; 1921 *Lustreware and Fruit* cat. no. 384 and *Italian Pitcher and Fruit* cat. no. 387; 1926 *Pottery and Fruit* cat. no. 184; 1930 *Still Life Interior* cat. no. 405

Born in Leesburg. Studied PAFA and with Bouguereauy, Ferrier, and Doucet in Paris. Taught at the PAFA. Associate member of the NAD. Founded the Darby Art School in 1900, later moving to Fort Washington, PA, to his home called Phloxedale.

BRIDGES, Fidelia (1835-1923)
> Exh. PAFA, 1905 *Wild Roses* cat. no. 820

Born in Salem, Mass., a pupil of W. T. Richards. Lived in Philadelphia in 1859 and 1862-63. Visited Europe in 1865-66, returned to live in Philadelphia 1879-80. Exhibited in 1865 a painting *Ferns* which belonged to Mrs. J. Haseltine, and in 1866 two paintings, *Violets*, which belonged to her fellow still life artist, R. M. Towne, and *Study from Nature*.

92

BROOKS, Cora Smalley (?-1930)
> Exh. PAFA, 1913 *Still Life* cat. no. 464; 1918 *Darwin Tulips* cat. no. 174 and *Rhododendrons* cat. no. 223; 1921 *September Flowers* cat. no. 76; 1925 *Peonies* cat. no. 202

BROWNELL, Matilda Auchinloss
> Exh. PAFA, 1906 *Still Life* cat. no. 318

She was born in New York.

BRYANT, Everett L.
> Exh. PAFA, 1914 *Peonies and Iris* cat. no. 336 and *Roses and Fan* cat. no. 420; 1915 *Gladioli* cat. no. 353, *Wild Phlox and Wild Lilies* cat. no. 402, *Peonies* cat. no. 528, and *Asters and Little Chrysanthemums* cat. no. 532; 1916 *Still Life* cat. no. 293; 1917 *Petunias* cat. no. 238; 1920 *Peonies and White Roses* cat. no. 109, *Asters* cat. no. 152, *Asters in Red Vase* cat. no. 154, *Snapdragons* cat. no. 211, and *White Phlox* cat. no. 241; 1922 *Dahlias* and *Petunias* cat. no. 298 and *Cloisonne and Chrysanthemums* cat. no. 319; 1923 *Dahlias and Petunias* cat. no. 333

BRYANT, Maude Drein
> Exh. PAFA, 1915 *The Bouquet* cat. no. 113, *Calendulas and Ceramics* cat. no. 121, and *Wild Azaleas and Iris* cat. no. 505; 1916 *Green and Rose* cat. no. 29 and *Vermillion, Rose and Blue* cat. no. 269; 1917 *June Basket* cat. no. 384; 1918 *Porcelains, Roses and Lacquer* cat. no. 454; 1922 *The Three Bouquets* cat. no. 280

BURR, Eliza J.
> Exh. PAFA, 1823 two watercolors

Sunbury, Pa. These were also exhibited by the artist when she moved to New York in 1842 at the American Institute of the City.

BURT, Jean Barde
> (1203 Walnut St., Philadelphia)
> Exh. PAFA, 1888 *Study of Geraniums* cat. no. 52

Born in Pennsylvania. Studied in Ladies' Decorative Art Club, PAFA, and under William Sartain.

BUTLER, Mary
> Exh. PAFA, 1927 *Poppies* cat. no. 28

CAMPIDOGLIO
> Exh. PAFA, 1876 *Fruit and Flowers* cat. no. 180; 1878, *Fruit* cat. no. 8

CARLES, Arthur B. (1882-1952)
> Exh. PAFA, 1905 *Still Life* cat. no. 873; 1918 *Still Life* cat. no. 314; 1920 *Roses* cat. no. 254 and *Bouquet* cat. no. 258; 1921 *Tulips* cat. no. 357; 1923 *Calla Lilies* cat. no. 251 and *Flowers in a Yellow Vase* cat. no. 306; 1930 *Still Life* cat. no. 335 and *Still Life* cat. no. 348

CHALFANT, Jefferson David (1856-1931)
> (Wilmington, Del.)
> Exh. PAFA, 1886 *Music, Still Life* cat. no. 41; 1888 *Violin and Music—Still Life* cat. no. 63; 1899 *Still Life* cat. no. 452

Born in Pennsylvania. Self-taught. Member Delaware Society of Artists. The artist was influenced by William Michael Harnett.

## CLARK, Thomas Shields
> (P. O. Box 1073, Pittsburg, Pa.)
> Exh. PAFA, 1892 *Sketch — Roses* cat. no. 36

Born in Pittsburg, 1860. Studied at Princeton University, Ecole des Beaux-Arts, Paris, Florence, and Venice. Member, American Artist Club, Paris. Honorable Mention, International Exhibition, Berlin.

## CLEMENT, Gabrielle de Veaux
> Exh. PAFA, 1927 *Summer Roses* cat. no. 270

## COHEN, Benjamin
> (West Chester, Pa.)
> Exh. PAFA, 1886 *An Onion Study* cat. no. 50

Born 1869 at St. John's, New Brunswick. Pupil of Carl Weber.

## COPE, George (1855-1929)
Born in 1855 to Caleb Swayne Cope and Lydia Eldridge Cope at the family farm which was on the Downington and West Chester State Road at the junction of Taylor's Mill Road with Copeland School Road. His father was a poet of some local repute whose work appeared in the Daily Local News. A paternal grandmother, a Swayne family which was noted in the art annals of Chester County, also encouraged Cope as a boy. George's older brother Nathan is said to have given the artist his first instruction in drawing. During his youth, the artist's efforts were, it is said, more directed towards efforts with his brush than towards the traditional school arts. He died in West Chester, Pa.

## CUNNINGHAM, Mary J.
> (Newton, Pa.)
> Exh. PAFA, 1890 *Roses* cat. no. 43

Studied at PAFA and with William Sartain.

## CUSHING, Howard Gardiner
> Exh. PAFA, 1915 *Spirea and Single Dahlias* (illus.) cat. no. 477, *Peonies* cat. no. 475, *Green Vase* cat. no. 480, and *Dahlias* cat. no. 560

## DARRAH, Ann Sophia Towne (1819-1881)
Born in Philadelphia September 30, 1819, the artist died in Boston. Sister of Rosalba M. Towne. Exhibited at the PAFA, as well as the Boston Athenaeum 1855-1865. Living in Philadelphia in 1856, she moved to Boston by 1867. Her husband, Robert K. Darrah, was employed by the U. S. Appraiser's Office in Boston.

## DAVIDS, Dorothy Lauer (1905-1980)
Born in York, Pa. she died in Latrobe, Pa. Dorothy Lauer Davids' family was Pennsylvania-German and she grew up in their substantial home in downtown York, Pennsylvania. She attended Edinboro College and was graduated in 1926. She married Paul Davids that same year and they settled in Greensburg, Pennsylvania. She later attended Seton Hill College and then took painting courses at Carnegie Institute of Technology (now Carnegie-Mellon University) where she studied with Samuel Rosenberg and Roy Hilton. She was a frequent exhibitor with the Associated Artists of Pittsburgh and the Mid-Year Show at the Butler Institute of American Art in Youngstown, Ohio. A travelling exhibition of her work was organized in the early 1930's and it was shown in a number of museums throughout the country. In 1933 Dorothy Davids and her husband Paul, Alex Fletcher, Mary A. Hornish and Mrs. Margie C. Bell met at the home of Julia B. Ulery on Otterman Street in Greensburg and organized the first Greensburg Community Art Exhibition. From 1935 to this date it has been known as the Greensburg Art Club. She was an exhibitor at the Greensburg Art Club's annual exhibitions until she stopped painting around 1951. In 1952 she became the manager of the Greensburg Antique Show which was first shown at the Armory and then the No. 1 Fire House and later at the old Buick Garage on Maple Avenue. From 1956 it became an annual event at Mountain View Inn. She was a competent violinist and collected widely in the field of American antiques.

## DAVIS, Stuart (1894-1964)
Davis was born in Philadelphia, and was a student of Robert Henri. The Armory Show in 1913 opened his eyes to the new painting being done in Europe and became one of the foremost abstractionists and cubists of this country.

## DeBEET, Cornelius De (ca. 1772-1840)
Born in Germany, but active in Philadelphia and Baltimore by 1812. Exhibited *Still Life of Fruit and Flowers* at the PAFA in 1812 and subsequently, as well as *Dead Game, Fruit,* and *Flowers* in 1832. Was said to be working in Philadelphia in 1812.

## DEIGENDESCH, Herman
> (9 N. 13th St., Philadelphia)
> Exh. PAFA, 1888 *Still Life* cat. no. 93

## DEMMLER, Fred A. (1888-1918)
Demmler was born in Manchester (Pittsburgh), Pa., and died 1918, Belgian Front, WW I. Much is known about Frederick Adolph Demmler, who was a native of Pittsburgh.

Demmler was one of eight children. His father was a prosperous businessman; he co-headed the kitchen equipment firm of Demmler and Schenck. Demmler's maternal grandfather established himself as an accomplished sculptor. The painter's other grandfather was a metals-working immigrant. He made the lanterns for the first gas lights to illuminate Pittsburgh streets.

Young Demmler attended public schools and graduated from Allegheny High-School in 1907, where he had been a student and close friend of the writer Willa Cather.

He studied later at the H.S. Stevenson Art School, then went to Cornell for two years. Next he took classes under Frank W. Benson and Edmund Tarbell at the Museum of Fine Arts School in Boston. Demmler showed paintings in the Associated Artists of Pittsburgh's annual exhibits between 1913 and 1918. His early paintings were still lifes and landscapes.

In 1914, he had work in the 18th Annual Exhibit (the forerunner of the Carnegie International). In June of the same year, Demmler sailed for Europe, expecting a year's study. The trip was cut short by the outbreak of war, so he returned to Pittsburgh. He chose Pittsburgh because his family was there, and because in Pittsburgh there were few painters to influence him. He said, "I stand more of a chance of being myself." Also he wished to avoid the social politics he had observed in the artistic circles of Boston. He had a shy personality and dressed as a businessman rather than an artist.

Demmler lived a short life, and by now he was painting the portraits that are associated with his later years. Demmler's later works in oil include three self-portraits and portraits of friends, along with portraits of local notables.

He was drafted for WW I, as were two of his brothers. Demmler said he would serve so that someone else did not have to go in his place. He was offered a chance to paint camouflage and thus avoid combat, but he rejected that offer and joined a machine gun battalion. He was made a sergeant.

In the final days of the war, the artist died of a wound inflicted by a high explosive shell on the Belgian front. At the time of his death, his paintings were on view in the Associated Artists' show.

DEMUTH, Charles (1883-1935)

Born and died in Lancaster, Pa. One of the masters of American watercolor, Demuth studied from 1899 to 1901 at Franklin & Marshall Academy in Lancaster after which he moved to Philadelphia to study art at Drexel Institute. He entered the Pennsylvania Academy of Fine Arts in 1905 where he studied for five years with William Merritt Chase, Thomas Anshutz, and Hugh Breckenridge, interrupted by a brief trip to Paris in 1909. A longer stay abroad, 1912 to 1914, allowed him to study at the Moderne, Colarossi, and Julian Academies but, most importantly, brought him into contact with Leo and Gertrude Stein. Through them he met Picasso, Juan Gris, and Robert Delaunay and learned from their Cezanne and Matisse paintings. He returned to the United States and

had his first one-man show of watercolors at New York's avant-garde Daniel Gallery.

In 1916-17, Demuth visited Bermuda with Marsden Hartley and began a series of watercolors, mostly landscapes, that reveal his first-hand awareness of Cubism. At the same time, Demuth's literary interests provided inspiration for a series of watercolor illustrations dramatically different in style and temperament. Not intended for publication, the paintings reflect negative aspects of human nature based on the writing of Zola, Henry James, and Poe. Demuth also did a great many flower and still life paintings which began in the expressionist style of his illustrations but later became more restrained and quiet. After about 1918, he placed them within a Cubist-based composition, although the organic vitality of the flowers continued to dominate and was the basis for a delicate faceting of the space surrounding them. His technique was always controlled, carefully considered and balanced in spontaneity and conception. One of the first Americans to adopt the industrial landscape as a theme, Demuth's work is considered the foundation for the Precisionist movement in this country.

DICKINSON, Preston (1891-1930)
    Exh. PAFA, 1924
His dealer was the Daniel Gallery in New York.

DUFFY, Mrs. E. B.
    Exh. PAFA, 1865, 1867, 1868, all for sale. *Fruit, Grapes, Flowers.*
In 1867 she is listed as living in Woodbury, N. J. Her address of 1865 is 2305 Coates St. and for 1868, 544 N. 4th St.

DUFFY, John B. (1828/29-after 1876)
In autumn 1866 the romantically titled paintings, *The Last Flower in Autumn* and the *First Flowers in Spring*, were exhibited by Duffy.

EAKINS, Susan H. MacDowell (1851-1938)
Born and died in Philadelphia, Pa. Susan H. MacDowell Eakins was overshadowed by her famous husband, Thomas Eakins. She was an accomplished painter, pianist, and amateur photographer.

EBBINGHOUSEN, Lavinia
    (1334 Chestnut St., Philadelphia)
    Exh. PAFA, 1888 *Study of Onions* cat. no. 113.
Studied at PAFA.

EDDOWES, Martha
    Exh. PAFA, 1813 *Flowers and Landscapes* painted on velvet

ENGSTROM, A. B.
Living in Philadelphia and exhibiting still life painting

94

from 1829 to 1845, his paintings were sometimes executed in watercolor and were noted as "from nature." In 1842, he exhibited *Still Life Pineapples* at the AFS. Engstrom is also listed as the owner of a still life, *Fruit Piece* by James Peale, exhibited at the AFS in 1845.

## EYERS, John J.

(108 S, 4th St., Philadelphia)
Exh. PAFA, 1868, all for sale. Two of *Game* and two of *Fruit*.

In 1869, there is a further exhibition by a J. W. Eyer of *Grapes*, now the property of A. K. McClure.

## FABER, Cornelia

(2039 Brandywine St., Philadelphia)
Exh. PAFA, 1888 *Hollyhocks* cat. no. 117 and *Wistaria* cat. no. 118

Studied at PAFA.

## FERGUSON, Margaret J. (1865-?)

(5200 Lancaster Ave., Philadelphia)
Exh. PAFA, 1886 *Still Life* cat. no. 91; 1889 *Still Life* cat. no. 68

Born in Philadelphia, 1229 N. 52d, 1865. Student at Spring Garden Institute.

## FITE, Mary

(2236 Fitzwater St., Philadelphia)
Exh. PAFA, 1885 *Rhododendrons* cat. no. 99

Studied at PAFA.

## FLETCHER, Alex (1866-1952)

Born in Elginshire, Scotland and died in Greensburg, Pa.

Alex Fletcher was born in Scotland, the son of Alexander and Anne Gair Fletcher. In his youth, he was apprenticed to an interior decorator named John Alves. His training partly included the cleaning and repairing of old oil portraits in the many castles and manor houses near his home. Fletcher served five years as an apprentice, then went on to study his trade in a professional school, the Mechanics' Institute.

In 1888, when Fletcher was twenty-two, he came to America. He lived in Mount Pleasant, but soon settled in Greensburg. There he shortly married a Greensburg native, Edna Bassett. In 1903, the artist moved his young wife and daughter to California for reasons of health. However, in 1906 the Fletcher family returned to Greensburg where they remained permanently.

An interior decorator by trade over a large part of his active career, Fletcher painted and decorated furniture, toys and various household articles for his customers. In addition to these tasks, he created flower paintings and views of gardens as he saw them around Greensburg. He also painted local scenes and landscapes.

Not trained to be a fine artist, Fletcher's work is in the tradition of American "naive" or "primitive" painters such as Grandma Moses and the Pittsburgh painter John Kane, whom Fletcher knew well. Fletcher's art reflects his gentle, likeable character. He once said, "I gained most of my knowledge about painting by attending art shows."

In his later years, the local scene definitely commanded his attention. An excellent example of his interest in Greensburg is his fine painting of the First Presbyterian Church.

Fletcher helped found the Greensburg Art Club; he was president of that organization from 1931 until 1949. For twenty-six years he was also a member of the Associated Artists of Pittsburgh. In 1942, the Greensburg Art Club honored him with a one-man show.

## FOERSTER, Emil (1822-1906)

Emil Foerster was born in Giessen, Germany in 1822 and moved to Pittsburgh, Pennsylvania with his bride in 1849. The artist returned briefly to Europe to study at Dusseldorf and then established his studio on Penn Avenue in Pittsburgh. Foerster remained in Pittsburgh until his death in 1906.

In 1859 Foerster exhibited three family portraits at the *First Annual Exhibition of the Pittsburgh Art Association*, including the group portrait of his own family, now in the collection of the Cathedral of Learning, University of Pittsburgh.

## FRANCIS, John F. (1808-1886)

(1840, Corner Library and 4th; 1841, 177 Quen St.; 1847, Harrisburg; 1855, near Wilmington, Del.; 1858, Phoenixville, PA.)

Born in Philadelphia, Pa., and died in Jeffersonville, Pa. Although his early training is unknown, Francis worked as an itinerant portrait painter in a number of small Pennsylvania towns in the 1830's and 40's. Beginning about 1850, he turned his attention to still life and specialized in creating American versions of the traditional Dutch "luncheon piece." He had a limited repertoire of objects which he skillfully used in variations of a few set compositions. His scenes were most often of dessert foods such as the fruits, nuts, cakes, bisquits, liquers and wines depicted in *Fruit and Wine*. In its complexity and richness, this painting is probably his masterpiece. It includes a view of a gently rolling landscape through a window behind the table, a device used in his most ambitious compositions. Painted in meticulous detail in the tradition of the work of the Peale family, he catches the reflection of light from the glasses and bottles, contrasted with the texture of orange peel and nuts. Characteristic of Francis' style is the high key, almost pastel color of this painting.

Francis exhibited in the Pennsylvania Academy of Fine Arts Annuals in 1847, 55 and 59 and many of his fruit pieces were sold through the American Art Union. He lived in Jeffersonville from 1866 to 86 but there are no known paintings by him after 1879.

95

FRANSSEN, Miss Annie
> (2001 Pine, Philadelphia)
> Exh. PAFA, 1889 *Fruit* cat. no. 74 and *Study of Onions* cat. no. 75

Born in Philadelphia. Student at PAFA.

GALVAN, Mrs. S. M.
> Exh. PAFA, 1878 *Roses* cat. no. 197

GARA, Calista Ingersoll

Married to the editor of the Erie Gazette, Isaac B. Gara. Primarily a portrait painter and teacher in Erie, PA, she was vice-president of the newly formed Erie Art Club in 1898. In 1860, she exhibited *The Pride of the Vineyard* which may have been a still life.

GEORGE, Miss
> Exh. PAFA, 1814 *Flowers*

GILCHRIST, JR., W. W.
> Exh. PAFA, 1906 *Still Life* cat. no. 518; 1909 *Creton Rose* cat. no. 10

GILMAN, Ben. Ferris
> (206 S. 36th St., Philadelphia)
> Exh. PAFA, 1890 *Roses* cat. no. 69 and *Daisies* cat. no. 70; 1892 *Peonies* cat. no. 98; 1895 *Still Life* cat. no. 129 and *Geraniums* cat. no. 130; 1900 *Peonies* cat. no. 203

Born in Salem, N.Y. In 1890, he lived at 204 S. 36th; studied at Ecole des Beaux Arts, Paris, and with Cabanel. He was at 1523 Chestnut St. in 1892.

GILMAN, Mrs. C. B.
> (1604 Summer St., Philadelphia)
> Exh. PAFA, 1885 *Les Chrysanthémes* cat. no. 111 and *Les Narcisses* cat. no. 112

Born at Steubenville, Ohio. Studied at PAFA and in Paris with Carolus-Duran.

GILMAN, Claude S.
> (1523 Chestnut, Philadelphia)
> Exh. PAFA, 1891 *Roses* cat. no. 101

Pupil of Henner and Carolus-Duran.

GLACKENS, William
> Exh. PAFA, 1925 *Field Flowers* cat. no. 206 and *Flowers in a Blue Vase* cat. no. 207

Born in Philadelphia, Pa., and died in Westport, Conn. Glackens worked as a newspaper illustrator in Philadelphia in the late 1890's while studying art at night at the Pennsylvania Academy of Fine Arts. There he became associated with the group of artists later called "The Eight" and the "Ashcan" painters who were working with Robert Henri to develop a spontaneous, realistic style of painting with contemporary life and people as their subject. His newspaper experience helped him develop a rapid sketching technique with incredible accuracy which later proved valuable in bringing spirit and immediacy to his paintings of early 20th century life.

Glackens went to Paris in 1895 with Henri but did not attend the French art schools preferring to capture the atmosphere of Parisian society in their own spontaneous sketches. 1896 marked Glackens' move to New York City where he continued to do illustration and began sending his paintings to Pennsylvania Academy exhibitions. Influenced by Henri and other painters in the realistic tradition, his early paintings tended to be low-keyed and sombre reflecting the mood of the city. A second trip to Europe in 1906 brought Glackens in contact with the work of Renoir which resulted in brighter color and a wider range of subjects in his subsequent work. Glackens participated in the 1908 exhibition of "The Eight" at MacBeth Gallery receiving acclaim for his masterpiece, *Chez Mouquin*. In 1912 he went abroad to help amass the now famous collection of Dr. Albert Barnes, a childhood friend. He spent two years painting in France 1925-27 then went back and forth to France until 1936 when his health began to decline.

GOODES, Edward Ashton (1832-1910)
> (1850, 460 Poplar; 1855, 12th St. and Poplar; 1864, 1217 Warnock St.; 1865, 639 Marshall St.; 1866-1868, 1217 Warnock, Philadelphia)
> Exh. PAFA, 1853 *Still Life, Music*

Goodes's father, an English tailor, came to America in 1829; Goodes was married to Anna Dobbins of Philadelphia in 1853. He is known to have painted portraits but as yet none have surfaced. His brother Ebenezer was also a painter and both were thought to have been engaged in the painting of signs for local fire companies and saloons.

GORSON, Aaron Henry (1872-1933)

Born in Kovno, Lithuania, and died in New York City. Gorson came to the United States at age 18 and began his training at the Pennsylvania Academy of Fine Arts in Philadelphia. He returned to Europe in 1899 and continued his education in Paris at the Julian Academy. In 1903 he opened a studio in Pittsburgh and made a specialty of painting scenes of the city's industry. He sought to provide the world with something new in his painting and felt Pittsburgh gave him that opportunity. A regular exhibitor at J. J. Gillespie Gallery in Pittsburgh and the Associated Artists of Pittsburgh, he was also a member of the American Art Association of Paris and the Union International des Beaux Arts et des Lettres, Paris.

GRANBERY, M. Lee
> (206 Sumac St., Wissahickon, Philadelphia)
> Exh. PAFA, 1891 *Ducks* cat. no. 105

Student at PAFA.

GRANBERY, Mollie L.
(Rochelle Ave., Wissahickon, Philadelphia)
Exh. PAFA, 1885 *Flowers of June* cat. no. 114

GRAVES, Miss L.
Exh. PAFA, 1876 *Panel of Roses* cat. no. 304

GRIDER, Rufus Alexander (1817-1900)
Born April 17, 1817, in Lititz, Pa. A member of the Moravian church, many of his studies are preserved in the Moravian Archives, Bethlehem, Pa. Lived in Bethlehem in 1854 when he sent four paintings for sale to the PAFA: *Amaryllis, Gladiolus, Flowers, Productions of Field and Forest in November, Forest Leaves in November,* and *White and Scarlet Roses, From Nature.* NYHS owns some studies of powder horns by this artist.

GRISWOLD, Carrissa A. (d. ca. 1879)
Exh. PAFA, 1866 *Flowers*; 1869, *Pineapples.* Both for sale.

GRONLAND, Theude (1817-1876)
In 1850, the firm of Goupil, Vibert, & Co. sent a still life by this artist to the PAFA for sale, *Still Life—Fish and Game.*

GROOMBRIDGE, William (1748-1811)
While living in Baltimore in 1811, Groombridge sent nine works for exhibition to the PAFA, of these four were still life paintings: *Peaches, A Melon, A Melon and Grapes,* and *Peaches.* All were listed as "For sale." In an 1812 supplemental catalog of the PAFA, there is a further still life, *Peaches,* exhibited by the artist. Born in Tunbridge, Kent, England, Groombridge was active in both London and in his native Kent from 1773 until 1790. Groombridge arrived in Philadelphia, probably in 1794, living there until 1804 when he moved to Baltimore where he died May 24, 1811. His wife Catherine conducted a girls' school in both cities.

HAILMAN, Johanna K. W. (1871-1958)
Exh. PAFA, 1913 *Oriental Poppies* cat. no. 57; 1919 *The Blue Jar* cat. no. 77; 1922 *September Flowers* cat. no. 297
Born in Pittsburgh, Pa., and died in Pittsburgh, Pa. Johanna Hailman was the daughter of distinguished Pittsburgh painter Joseph R. Woodwell, with whom she began her early training in art. She painted in the large studio on the Woodwell estate in Pittsburgh and at her winter home in Nassau and during her extensive travelling. Her work was exhibited in every Carnegie International except two from the first in 1896 until 1955. In 1915, Hailman was awarded a silver medal at the Panama-Pacific Exposition and was a member of the Committee of Selection for the 1924 International. Carnegie Institute presented a one-woman exhibition of her work in 1927. The majority of Hailman's subjects were derived from

her love of the outdoors, especially gardens. Many of her paintings depict scenes in the South and the West Indies with a number of watercolors of Nassau and Jamaica. She had numerous portrait commissions during her career, among them Douglas Stewart, a Director of the Department of Fine Arts, Carnegie Institute.

A dynamic individual, Hailman was an active and outspoken member of the Pittsburgh art scene and crusaded for beautification of the city as well.

HANCE, Emma A.
Exh. PAFA, 1886 *Study of Corn* cat. no. 110 and *Study of Roses* cat. no. 111; 1888 *Study of Chrysanthemums* cat. no. 153
Born and educated in Philadelphia, she was a pupil of Milne Ramsey.

HANSEL, Miss H. M.
(18 N. 6th St., Philadelphia)
Exh. PAFA, 1828 *A Vase with Flowers* and *Flowers, Water Lily*; 1829 *Flowers* (2) and *A Vase of Flowers,* all watercolors.

HANSELL, A. B.
Exh. PAFA, 1878 *Calla Lily* cat. no. 151

HARDY, JR., James (1832-1889)
Exhibited a group of *Dead Game Still Lifes* in watercolor for 1857, and also a painting called *Bird's Nest* which might have been in the style of William Henry Hunt who was popular at this time. The paintings exhibited belonged to C. J. Price & Co. and E. S. Clark.

HARNETT, William Michael (1848-1892)
William Michael Harnett was born in Clonakilty, county Cork, Ireland.

One of the most interesting revivals of our day is that of the still life, trompe l'oeil sytle, best exemplified by his work, a native of Philadelphia, where the tradition of the Peales was always alive. The smooth, skillfully painted "deceptions" of Harnett are startingly realistic.

HART, Jessie
(1020 Chestnut St., Philadelphia)
Exh. PAFA, 1886 *Pigeons* cat. no. 117 and *Snowballs* cat. no. 118
Born in Madison, Indiana. Studied at the Philadelphia School of Design for Women.

HASELTINE, Mrs. J.
Exh. PAFA, 1865 *Water-lilies*

HEADE, Martin Johnson (1819-1904)
(1847, Corner of Arch and 8th Sts.; 1856, Trenton, N. J.)
Heade did not exhibit any still life paintings at the PAFA. He was born in rural Pennsylvania and died in St. Augustine, Fla.

Landscape, portrait, and still life painter, Heade's intense love of nature and light is expressed with charm and delicacy in his art, and today his flower and bird paintings are most highly prized.

HEEBNER-McDONALD, Ann
Exh. PAFA, 1913 *Parrot Tulips* cat. no. 12

HELMOLD, Adele M.
(1334 Chestnut St., Philadelphia)
Exh. PAFA, 1885 *Snowballs* cat. no. 135; 1888 *Dollie* cat. no. 159 and *Chrysanthemums*; 1890 *Cherries* cat. no. 90 and *Oranges* cat. no. 91

Born in Philadelphia, she studied at the PAFA.

HENDERSON, Kelly J.
(21 S. 42nd St., Philadelphia)
Exh. PAFA, 1885 *Mallard Duck—Still Life* cat. no. 164

Born in Philadelphia. The artist studied at PAFA and was a member of the Sketch Club.

HERGESHEIMER, Ella S.
Exh. PAFA, 1906 *Still Life—Mushrooms* cat. no. 254

HETZEL, George (1826-1899)
(1855, Pittsburg; 1857, Penn St., Pittsburg; 1859-1869, Pittsburg)
Exh. PAFA, 1878 *Still Life—Quail* cat. no. 182 and *Still Life—Quail* cat. no. 251

Exhibits in 1855 a painting *Game: Turkey and Rabbit* for sale by the artist. Also *Game Rabbits and Birds* belonging to Joseph Harrison, as well as a *Still Life* for sale. 1863: *Dead Game* for sale by the artist. 1865: *Game* belonging to J. L. Claghorn and *Fruit* belonging to J. S. Martin. Hetzel's other exhibitions were for the most part landscapes of western Pennsylvania and a few game paintings such as *Ivory-billed Woodpecker*.

George Hetzel was born near Strasbourg, France, and died in Pittsburgh, Pa.

Hetzel moved to Pittsburgh with his family at age two. His parents encouraged his natural artistic talent and he received his first training as an apprentice to a house and sign painter. Income generated from painting interior decorations for the old Western Penitentiary and for several river boats and cafés, helped to finance two years of study at the Düsseldorf Academy 1847-49. Soon after his return to Pittsburgh, he painted portraits of his parents which reveal his facility with the precise, realistic style of painting for which Düsseldorf was then famous. His *Self Portrait* dates from this period and gives a mysterious and theatrical view of the artist. Dressed in black with full, dark beard, his image emerges from the shadow of a wide-brimmed hat, the paint surface smooth and even. He continued to do portraits and still lifes throughout his career but by the late 1850's was concentrating on landscapes of the western Pennsylvania area. At Scalp Level,

a mountain retreat outside the city, he painted with a congenial group of Pittsburgh artists in much the same way as did their French contemporaries at Barbizon. *Mifflin County Landscape* is an example of Hetzel's large yet quiet and intimate views of nature which sold almost as quickly as they were painted. His very detailed landscapes of the 1860's emphasizing textures and reflected light, gave way in the next decade to a freer style of brushwork. Toward the end of the century his style revealed a growing interest in depicting landscape in terms of light as a response to the Impressionist movement. *Paint Creek Road,* a view down a wooded, country road at Scalp Level, demonstrates Hetzel's ability to suggest warm sunlight and atmosphere with a delicate touch of bright color.

Hetzel was acclaimed as a portrait artist and his sensitivity to his sitters is apparent in the three-quarter length view of *Miss Helen Myers.* Once the sweetheart of Hetzel's brother, Miss Myers was married to William H. Allen in 1889 and was the mother of Hervey Allen, the author of *Anthony Adverse.* He presents her in a quiet, pensive mood, her delicate beauty accentuated by his careful rendering of her soft blue gown and white shawl. Each touch of the brush has an expressive naturalism reminiscent of the style of Thomas Eakins.

Painted in a more precisely realistic style is our small *Still Life.* Although a subject Hetzel painted throughout his career, few still lifes remain.

Hetzel was the only Pittsburgh artist represented at the 1876 Centennial Exhibition in Philadelphia. In 1893 he sent three paintings to the Chicago World's Fair and he participated in the first Carnegie International in 1896. He taught at the Pittsburgh School of Design for Women from its inception in 1865 and frequently took his students to the country to paint from nature. His final years were spent at the farm house at Somerset to which he had moved his family in 1897. Carnegie Institute presented a major retrospective exhibition of Hetzel's work in 1909, recognizing him as one of Pennsylvania's most significant artists.

HETZEL, George T. (1847?-1912)
George T. Hetzel was born in Pittsburgh, Pa., and died in Pittsburgh, Pa.

He was the nephew of George Hetzel, and painted most of his life in the area of New Castle and Slippery Rock, Pa. Hetzel worked in both watercolor and in oil doing mostly landscapes and still lifes. He died in Allegheny City at the age of 65.

HETZEL, Lila B. (1873-1967)
Lila B. Hetzel was born in Pittsburgh, Pa., and died in Somerset, Pa.

The youngest child of Pittsburgh artist George Hetzel, "Miss Lila," as she was affectionately known, began her career at her father's side when quite young and continued painting for over 70 years. At 16, she was the young-est student in the life class at the Pittsburgh School of Design where she studied for four years with Martin B. Leisser and David Walkley.

In 1897 Lila moved with her family to a large farm house in Somerset, Pa., where her father established a studio which she maintained following his death in 1899. Her early landscapes are in the tradition of George Hetzel and the Scalp Level artists and closely parallel his Barbizon influenced style. In later years she shifted to a more two-dimensional and less painterly approach in a series of interior views of the farm and studio called "Old Fashioned Corners." *Farm House Garrett* is one of these picturesque scenes of Americana painted in a realistic but not photographic style. In *Grouse Hanging on a Door*, she copied a *trompe l'oeil* composition of her father's, perhaps as a student exercise.

Lila Hetzel took a studio in Pittsburgh in 1909 where the Associated Artists of Pittsburgh was organized the following year. She was an active exhibitor and partici-pant in the artistic activities of the city and of the rural Somerset community between which she divided her time. She was married to William H. Kantner and her daughter Dorothy was an art critic in Pittsburgh and Somerset.

HEYL, Matilda C.
(2122 Walnut St., Philadelphia)
Exh. PAFA, 1885 *Basket of Peaches* cat. no. 143
She was a pupil of Milne Ramsey.

HIGGINS, Helen
(1710 N. 21st St., Philadelphia)
Exh. PAFA, 1888 *One the Half Shell* cat. no. 165
Studied at Philadelphia School of Design for Women.

HILL, J.
Exh. PAFA, 1854 *Fruit and Flowers*
Living at Noble Street below 8th in Philadelphia when he sent this painting for sale to the PAFA.

HOBBS, George Thompson (1846-?)
(1875, 804 8th St., Philadelphia)
Still life and landscape painter, he exhibited *Pansies* at NAD in 1875, 1879-82.

Studied at the Pennsylvania Academy of the Fine Arts and studied in Paris with Bouguereau and Tony Robert-Fleury. A painter and art restorer; painted landscapes, working in Philadelphia.

HOLD (Abel Hold?)
Exh. PAFA, 1858 *Bird's Nest*
This painting belonged to Charles Dey.

HOLME, Lucy D.
(1020 Chestnut St., Philadelphia)
Exh. PAFA, 1885 *Roses* cat. no. 147
Studied at PAFA, and with William Sartain. She is repre-sented in the Temple Collection, PAFA, and received the Mary Smith Prize, PAFA, 1884.

HOLMES, Mrs. G. W.
(1512 Chestnut St., Philadelphia)
Exh. PAFA, 1885 *Roses* cat. no. 148
Studied at PAFA, and with John Neagle and G. W. Holmes.

HOLYOKE (Wm. Holyoake, 1834-1894?)
Exh. PAFA, 1862 *Strawberries*
This painting was for sale and was the property of George Whitney.

HOOD, Mrs. Matilda
(1827, 51 Filbert St., Philadelphia)
Exhibited *Shells*, a watercolor.

HOPKINS, John (John Henry Hopkins, 1792-1868?)
Exh. PAFA, 1820 *Shells, Coral, and Weed*
Watercolors (two similar exhibited); they were also shown in a special exhibition in 1821.

HORTER, Earl (1883-1940)
Began his career as an engraver of stock certificates and later worked for Philadelphia's largest advertising agency, N. W. Ayer & Sons from 1917 through 1923. Later he became a free-lance illustrator which gave him time to pursue his non-commercial art. Horter studied etching under James Fincken (an instructor at the Graphic Sketch Club who was eventually succeeded by Horter) and was influenced by the work of Joseph Pennell and James Abbott McNeill Whistler. A frequent exhibitor at the PAFA watercolor exhibitions from 1915 until his death, he began in 1924 to show at the Academy's painting annu-als. Success in his commercial career enabled him to tra-vel abroad where he was greatly influenced by European modernism and to assemble a collection of avant-garde French paintings. In 1934 his collection was shown at the Philadelphia Museum of Art and the Arts Club of Chicago. Included were works by his artist colleagues from Philadelphia, Arthur B. Carles and Charles Sheeler, as well as seventeen Picassos (including his important Cubist work, *L'Arlesienne*), ten Georges Braques, and Henry Matisse's *Italian Women* of 1915; in addition, he owned Constantine Brancusi's marble of *Mademoiselle Pogany* of 1910 and an oil study of Marcel Duchamp's *Nude Descending a Staircase*. Horter's home in central Philadelphia became an important outpost for early modernism. During the latter part of his life, he spent much of his time as a teacher, first at the Graphic Sketch Club and later at the

Tyler School of Art at Temple University. The Philadelphia Art Alliance mounted a memorial exhibition of his work after his death at the age of 56.

HOVENDEN, Thomas (1840-1895)
(Plymouth Meeting, Montgomery Co., PA)
Born in Dunmanway, County Cork, Ireland. He studied in the Cork School of Design, NAD, New York, and the Ecole des Beaux-Arts, Paris. Member of the Society of American Artists, American Watercolor Society, New York Etching Club, and the Philadelphia Society of Artists. A sentimental genre painter, his accomplishment as a craftsman was notable, and perhaps his greatest effectiveness was in teaching. Robert Henri was one of his students.

HOWELL, Edward A. (1848-1924)
Worked in Reading, Pa.

HUMPHREYS, Albert (1863-?)
(1622 Cherry St., Philadelphia)
Exh. PAFA, 186? *Group of Vases* cat. no. 136
Born in Cincinnati, she was a graduate of the School of Design, University of Cincinnati. Studied at PAFA and was a member of the Philadelphia Sketch Club.

HUNT, Mrs. Jane M.
Exh. PAFA, 1867 *Flowers and Water Lily.* Both for sale.

HUNZINGER, William (Werner?)
Exh. PAFA, 1863 *Grapes*
This painting was owned by George Whitney, New York.

JENKINS, Mrs. H. Tempest
(1328 Chestnut, Philadelphia)
Exh. PAFA, 1891 *Laughing Potatoes* cat. no. 162, *Mussels* cat. no. 163, and *Still Life* cat. no. 164; 1899 *Still Life* cat. no. 456
Born in Philadelphia, she studied in Paris, and with H. Thompson at Puteaux.

JOHNSON, F. Morton
Exh. PAFA, 1908 *Still Life* cat. no. 315; 1910 *Still Life* cat. no. 680
(MMA catalogue notes, in pencil, say "good study of white china on white cloth," refers to no. 315.)

JOHNSON, H. (Probably Mary Ann Johnson QV)

JOHNSON, Mary Ann
Exh. PAFA, 1867 *Vase of Flowers, Pansies, China Aster, Tulips,* and *Peaches.* All for sale.

JUSTICE, Elizabeth B.
(1520 Chestnut St., Philadelphia)
Exh. PAFA, 1886 *Still Life* cat. no. 145
Born in Philadelphia, she studied at PAFA, and under William Sartain and F. A. Bridgman.

KEAST, Susette
Exh. PAFA, 1923 *Chinese Still Life* cat. no. 325

KING, Albert F. (1854-1945)
Albert F. King was born in Pittsburgh in 1854. He studied with Martin B. Leisser who was also his friend. A popular and familiar figure to Pittsburghers of his time, King excelled at portraiture, but was known to paint landscapes, still lifes and genre scenes occasionally, mostly for his own pleasure. He made his living as an artist by doing portraits of the city's bank presidents and business officials. Many of the portraits of distinguished Pittsburghers done by King hung in the Duquesne Club, of which he also was a member. "King gets the best likeness," was the explanation of those who commissioned him. He maintained a studio in the Stevenson Building, Pittsburgh, and when not engaged in a portrait commission, spent his time painting likenesses from old tintypes. A portrait of Stephen Foster in his early twenties was done by King in this manner from an old tintype in the Foster Memorial. Included in this exhibition is a portrait of George Hetzel that he did from a photograph.

Except for a period of years spent at the Omaha, Nebraska home of one of his sons, "Al" King worked in Pittsburgh all of his life. He gave an interview to art critic Dorothy Kantner of the *Pittsburgh Sun-Telegraph* in 1938 after which she wrote, "Today, at 83, the Pittsburgh painter (King) is still one to whom many turn for portrait work. His hand is just as steady, his ability to secure a likeness just as infallible." Albert King died at the home of his son, Albert E. King, in Pittsburgh's East End, on February 4, 1945.

KLAF, Willem (1621/2-1693)
Exh. PAFA, 1815 *Fruit Piece*

KNEIPP, GEORG (1793-1862)
(92 N. 11th St., Philadelphia)
Exh. PAFA, 1854 *Fruit* and *Fruit*

KNOX, Anna
(2120 Race, Philadelphia)
Exh. PAFA, 1891 *Study of Grapes* cat. no. 175

KOLLOCK, Mary (1832/1840-1911)
(1864, Philadelphia; 1866, New York)
Exh. PAFA, 1864 Sculpture; 1866 *Vase of Flowers*

KRUSE, W. B.
(716 Buttonwood, Philadelphia)
Exh. PAFA, 1889 *Fruit*
The artist studied at PAFA.

LADD, Laura D. S.
Exh. PAFA, 1928 *Still Life and Dahlias* cat. no. 160, awarded the Mary Smith Prize; 1930 *Flowers and Interior* cat. no. 48

100

LAMBDIN, George C. (1830-1896)
Exh. PAFA, 1876 *Roses* cat. no. 56; 1885 *The Secret of the Rose* cat. no. 179 and *Roses in the Spring* cat. no. 182; 1888 *Flowers by a Window* cat. no. 200; 1905 *Autumn Leaves* cat. no. 117

Born in Pittsburgh, Lambdin went to Philadelphia to study under Thomas Sully, later returning to his home town as a portrait painter and proprietor of a museum and art gallery. He painted many national figures and also was a successful miniaturist.

Lewis Prang & Co. published flower paintings by Lambdin in chromolithography.

LANG, Annie Traquair
Exh. PAFA, 1912 *Still Life* cat. no. 62

LANGLEY, Sarah
Exh. PAFA, 1921 *Apples* cat. no. 370

LANING, William M. (fl. 1850s)
His birth and death dates are unknown. Painter of genre and still life; decorator and commercial artist. Working in Charleston, South Carolina 1837-8 with Giovanni Chizzola. In Philadelphia 1841-49 with a partner, R. G. Laning, house and sign painters. Baltimore in 1851-60 as a block letterer and ornamental painter. Laning with different initials WS and WL exhibited genre and still life paintings at the Maryland Historical Society in 1853 and 1856.

LAWLER, Martin J. (active 1870-1889)
Lawler painted in and around Erie, Pa., in the late 1870s. He was painting fruit pieces but later turned to illusionistic works in the style of Harnett.

LAWMAN, Jasper Holman (1825-1906)
Born in Xenia, Ohio and died in Pittsburgh, Pa. In 1839, while working in Cincinnati, Lawman painted a riverboat scene which drew such attention that a group of friends offered to send him to Europe to study art. Instead he ended up in Pittsburgh in 1846 and became a scene painter at the old Drury Theatre. His European trip was realized in 1859 when he left for Paris to study portraiture with Thomas Couture. After a period of travel, he returned to Pittsburgh and established himself as a portraitist. Andrew Carnegie, William Negley, and banker John Harper were among those whose likeness he painted during his long career.

As an active Pittsburgh artist, Lawman probably joined local painters on summer sketching trips to Scalp Level, a popular mountain retreat for area artists near Somerset.

LAWRENCE, Christopher Ludwig
Born in Hamburg, Germany, he changed his name from Leverentz. He was a follower of Severin Roesen.

LEAVITT, Emma F.
(1334 Chestnut St., Philadelphia)
Exh. PAFA, 1885 *Roses* cat. no. 189

LEISSER, Martin B. (1846-1940)
Born in Pittsburgh, Pa. and died in Pittsburgh, Pa. Gaining his initial training in art from older Pittsburgh artists including George Hetzel, Leisser was able to go abroad after the Civil War and studied at the Julian Academy in Paris and at the Academy in Munich. Although he always preferred landscapes, he established a successful portrait career on his return to Pittsburgh in order to earn his living. Leisser was devoted to encouraging young area artists and served as Headmaster of the Pittsburgh School of Design and introduced the first life modeling classes in the city. He became a close friend of Andrew Carnegie and was influential in convincing Carnegie to include an art school in Carnegie Institute of Technology (now Carnegie-Mellon University). As one of the major figures in the Pittsburgh art world for over 50 years, Leisser was a founder of the Art Society of Pittsburgh and served on the original Fine Arts Committee for Carnegie Institute. A note in the artist's hand on the reverse of the landscape in this collection, identifies the location depicted as the Adirondack woods around the home of Mrs. Lucy Carnegie. Sketched in a free, very painterly technique, it is an intimate view of a cool, green forest in summer. The foliage is dense and the sun gently flickers through the branches to the damp earth. The painting delights in the quiet beauty of nature and has the freshness and life of some of the small, nature studies by Pittsburgh artists, George Hetzel and Joseph Woodwell done at Scalp Level, a remote mountain village and frequent gathering place for Pittsburgh artists.

At his death, the Leisser Art Fund was established from his estate to provide purchase awards and scholarships for artists in Pittsburgh and Munich.

LESLEY, Margaret W. (1857-?)
(1008 Clinton St., Philadelphia)
Exh. PAFA, 1885 *Rosebuds* cat. no. 193

Born in Philadelphia. She studied at PAFA, and in Paris under Jules Lefebvre and Boulanger.

LEUTZE, Emmanuel Gottlieb (1816-1868)
The Philadelphia artist enrolled in the Düsseldorf Academy in 1841, where he established a large studio which became a center of activity for his fellow Americans, among them Worthington Whittredge and Eastman Johnson. By 1859 the artist returned to America from his residence in Dusseldorf. Perhaps his most important painting would be *Washington Crossing the Delaware*, (The Metropolitan Museum of Art).

**LEWIS, Samuel**
>(1811, Philadelphia; 1812-1817, Race St. near 10th St., Philadelphia)
>Exh. PAFA, 1811 *A Deception*

**LIPPINCOTT, Margarette (1862-?)**
>(1637 Girard Ave.; 1334 Chestnut St., Philadelphia)
>Exh. PAFA, 1885 *Roses* cat. no. 204; 1886 *Daisies* cat. no. 164; 1892 *Roses* cat. no. 149 and *Geraniums* cat. no. 150; 1893 *White Roses* cat. no. 54

Born in Philadelphia, she studied at PAFA, Art Students League, and with George C. Lambdin and Joseph DeCamp.

**LOEB, Bella M. (1870-?)**
>(2124 Spring Garden St., Philadelphia)
>Exh. PAFA, 1886 *Study of Corn* cat. no. 167

Born in Philadelphia.

**LOESER, Elizabeth**
>(1417 N. 16th St., Philadelphia)
>Exh. PAFA, 1889 *Still Life* cat. no. 138

Born in Pottsville.

**LOGUE, John James (ca. 1810-after 1864)**
>(1840, Library St.; 1853, GoodWill between Race and Vine Sts.; 1854-1857, 7 Lybrand St.; 1859-1864, 223 Lybrand St., Philadelphia)
>Exh. PAFA, 1876 *Grapes* cat. no. 162

In 1848 Logue shows *Letter and Pen*, a miniature; 1854-57 he exhibits at least one still life; in 1859, *A Choice Desert*. He continues to exhibit still lifes through 1868. Logue worked in Philadelphia and was an extremely prolific painter of still lifes.

**LOGUE, Kate**
>Exh. PAFA, 1853 *Flowers*, watercolor

**LOWNES, Anna**
>(Media, Pa; 1708 Chestnut St., Philadelphia)
>Exh. PAFA, 1885 *Still Life* cat. no. 209 and *Yellow Roses* cat. no. 210; 1888 *Carnations* cat. no. 216; 1890 *Study of Apples* cat. no. 116 and *Study of Wild Azalea* cat. no. 117

She was a pupil of Milne Ramsey in 1885.

**LUKS, George Benjamin (1867-1933)**
Born in Williamsport, Pa. and died in New York City. Luks began his career studying at the Pennsylvania Academy of Fine Arts in Philadelphia and then from 1885 to 1891 he travelled and studied in Düsseldorf, Munich and Paris. While abroad he was impressed with the work of Renoir and Manet and especially Frans Hals whose style greatly influenced Luks in developing his own spontaneous approach to painting. He worked for several years as a newspaper cartoonist and illustrator in Philadelphia and New York which brought him into con-tact with the group of young artists around Robert Henri later to be called "The Eight." Like other members of this group, Luks sought to paint the events and people he encountered in the city with a vibrating sense of life. He exhibited with "The Eight" at MacBeth Gallery in 1908 and at the Armory Show in 1913. He taught at the Art Students League in New York from 1920 to 1924 and at his own school from 1924 to 1933.

**MAAS, Jacob (ca. 1800-?)**
>Exh. PAFA, 1834 *Flowers and Insects*

**MacDOWELL, Miss S. H.**
>Exh. PAFA, 1878 *The Picture Book* cat. no. 248

**MACHEN, W. H.**
>Exh. PAFA, 1876 *Ducks and Teal* cat. no. 283

**MAGILL, Beatrice (1859-?)**
>(Providence, R.I.; 1420 Chestnut St., Philadelphia)
>Exh. PAFA, 1885 *Chrysanthemums* cat. no. 214; 186? *Chrysanthemums* cat. no. 172; 1890 *Hydrangeas* cat. no. 120 and *Poppies* cat. no. 121

Born in Swarthmore, PA, she studied at PAFA and under William Sartain; in Paris, under Feyen-Perrin.

**MANSON, M.**
>Exh. PAFA, 1821 *Flowers on silk*, a theorem painting

**MARIO, Allesandro**
>Exh. PAFA, 1868 *Raspberries*

The painting was owned by Jay Cooke.

**MARRK**
>Exh. PAFA, 1814 *Flowers*

**MARSHALL, Mary E.**
>Exh. PAFA, 1926 *New England Flowers* cat. no. 124

**MARTEL**
>Exh. PAFA, 1815 *Fruit Piece*

**MASON, Mary Townsend**
>Exh. PAFA, 1921 *Tulips* cat. no. 422; 1922 *Iris and Azaleas* cat. no. 288, *Miss Lingard and Phlox* cat. no. 301 and *Still Life with Fruit* cat. no. 302, awarded the Mary Smith Prize; 1923 *Della Robbia* cat. no. 340; 1925 *Zinnias* cat. no. 24 and *Peonies* cat. no. 188; 1926 *Silver Moon Roses* cat. no. 122 and *Island Flowers* cat. no. 259; 1927 *Flowers in Light* cat. no. 311; 1928 *Krisheim Tulips* cat. no. 69; 1929 *September Flowers* cat. no. 32; 1930 *Peonies* cat. no. 18

**MASON, William (d. ca. 1840)**
>(1814, Norris's Alley, Philadelphia; 1830-1838, 27 Sanson St.; 1841, Sanson St. near 8th)
>Exh. AFS, 1838 *Fruit*, in crayons; 1841 *Still Life—Vegetables* and *Dead Game*, a watercolor
>Exh. PAFA, 1853 *Still Life*, property of W. H. Strickland

MATLACK, Eleanor
(1321 Walnut, Philadelphia)
Exh. PAFA, 1891 *Still Life* cat. no. 204
She was born in Philadelphia.

McCARTER, Henry Bainbridge (1864-1942)

McCLANE, Miss
Exh. PAFA, 1832 *Water Melon and Peaches*

McCLOSKEY, William J.
(American Tile Building, 140 W. 23rd, New York)
Exh. PAFA, 1889 *Florida Lemons* cat. no. 155
Born in Philadelphia, he studied at PAFA under Professors Schuessele and Eakins.

McCLURG, Trevor (1816-1893)
(1859, Pittsburg; 1861-69, New York)
Exh. PAFA, 1861 *Grapes and Fruit*
Trevor McClurg was born in Pittsburgh around 1816. After studying abroad in the 1840's, spending most of his time in Italy, he returned to the United States and lived in Pittsburgh continuously from 1848 to 1877. He exhibited in Philadelphia in 1845, 1859, 1861, and 1865, and exhibited in New York in 1846, 1848, 1853, and 1858. The catalogues of the Pittsburgh Artists Association shows him exhibiting in 1859, 1860, and 1871. McClurg was associated with the Scalp Level Group, though not primarily a landscape painter. He was a teacher at the School of Design for Women in Pittsburgh in the late 1860's. Although he was known for his many portraits, he also painted figure pieces and genre scences. He died in Asheville, North Carolina.

McDONALD, Ann Heebner
Exh. PAFA, 1920 *Still Life* cat. no. 296

McILWAINE, Mattie
(3445 Walnut St., Philadelphia)
Exh. PAFA, 1886 *Still Life* cat. no. 176
Student of Spring Garden Institute.

McNABB, Miss Kate
(108 Mill St., Germantown, Philadelphia)
Exh. PAFA, 1890 *Roses* cat. no. 127

MEER, John
(4 South 7th St., Philadelphia)
Exh. PAFA, 1812 *Still Life*

MEESER, Lillian B.
Exh. PAFA, 1918 *Rhododendrons* cat. no. 442; 1920 *The Blue Tea Pot* cat. no. 176, *Chrysanthemums* cat. no. 177, and *A Bowl of Flowers* cat. no. 179; *The Chinese Idol* cat. no. 351 and *Peonies* cat. no. 442; 1922 *Cloisonne and Chrysanthemums* cat. no. 316; 1925 *Fruits and Flowers* cat. no. 85, *Dahlias* cat. no. 87, and *Fall Blooms* cat. no. 204; 1927 *Things Oriental* cat. no. 78 and *The Old Belgian Bottle* cat. no. 328; 1928 *Still Life* cat. no. 179; 1929 *Zinnia and Petunia* cat. no. 17; 1930 *Still Life* cat. no. 115 and *Rhododendrons* cat. no. 522

MERRITT, Anna Lea

MIDDLETON, Mary P.
(Walnut Lane, Germantown, Philadelphia)
Exh. PAFA, 1892 *Japanese Persimmons* cat. no. 207

MIFFLIN, Lloyd (1846-1921)
Born in Columbia Pa., and known as both a poet and painter, Mifflin was the son of a professional painter, John Houston Mifflin. He studied in Philadelphia under Isaac Williams and Thomas Moran, and in Europe. In his early days he painted industriously, until 1872, when his health declined. After this date, he gave his time chiefly to poetry.

MIKEL, E. Ferti
Exh. PAFA, 1820 *Flowers—Roses, Marigolds, and Daffodils,* watercolor

MILLDER, Mildred B.
Exh. PAFA, 1925 *Flags and Darwin Tulips* cat. no. 180

MILLER, Henry
Pupil of Roesen, while living in Huntingdon, Pa.

MILLER, Minnie M.
Exh. PAFA, 1918 *Still Life* cat. no. 42 and *Flowers* cat. no. 264; 1921 *Still Life* cat. no. 214 and *Nasturtiums* cat. no. 330

MITCHELL, Edward M. (1831-1872)
(1864, 5 S. 6th St.; 1865, S. W. Corner 6th and Arch Sts.; 1868-69, 705 Wyatts St., Philadelphia)
Exh. PAFA, 1864 *Fruit*; 1868 *Tempting Morsels*

MITCHELL, Rosalie
(1125 Arch, Philadelphia)
Exh. PAFA, 1891 *California Peaches* cat. no. 210 and *French Strawberries* cat. no. 211
Born in Baltimore, she studied with Thomas Eakins, Philadelphia, and with J. P. Laurens and G. Courtois, Paris.

MOLARSKY, Morris
Exh. PAFA, 1915 *Still Life* cat. no. 333; 1923 *The Antique Fan* cat. no. 350

MOLYN, Marie
Exh. PAFA, 1878 *Flowers* cat. no. 58

MONNET-LAVERPILIERE, E.
Exh. PAFA, 1878 *Flowers* cat. no. 55

MORAN, Thomas (1837-1926)
One still life, collection of WHG.

MULHERN, William A.
Exh. PAFA, 1890 *Still Life* cat. no. 140
Spring Garden Institute

MURDAL, J.
Exh. PAFA, 1865 *Still Life*
The painting was owned by G. Eckert.

MURTLAND, M. M.
Exh. PAFA, 1876 *Grandfather's Bible* cat. no. 12

NATT, Phoebe D.
Exh. PAFA, 1876 *Peaches* cat. no. 300 and *Grapes* cat.
no. 301; 1886 *Dogwood Blossoms* cat. no. 191

NEAGLE, Miss E.
Exh. PAFA, 1819 *Moss Rose*, watercolor; *Flowers – Rose and
Tulip*, watercolor; 1822 *Flowers*

NEWMAN, Carl
Exh. PAFA, 1906 *Still Life* cat. no. 216

NEWTON, Mrs.
(Roxborough, Pa.)
Exh. PAFA, 1841 *Flowers – After Nature; Flowers – After Nat-
ure;* and *Flowers – After Nature.* All for sale.

NIEMANN, Elizabeth C.
(3405 Baring, Philadelphia)
Exh. PAFA, 1891 *Study of Tokay Grapes* cat. no. 222
Born in Philadelphia, she was a student in the School of
Design for Women.

NORRIS, S. Walter
Exh. PAFA, 1921 *Old Books* cat. no. 341

NORTH, Mary
(Cherry St. above 5th, north side; 1829, corner of Rasp-
berry Alley, in Race St.; 1840, Vine above 11th, Philadelphia)
Exh. PAFA, 1828 *Fruit and Flowers*

NOYES, George L.
Exh. PAFA, 1911 *Still Life* cat. no. 139

NUNES, Abraham I.
(Race St., Philadelphia)
Exh. PAFA, 1811 *A Deception*, drawing or watercolor; *View of
Lemon Hill, the Seat of Henry Pratt*

His birth and death dates are unknown. Portrait, landscape, and still life painter and a drawing master. In Philadelphia in 1810-1814, was an associate of the Society of
Artists, and exhibited in their 1811 exhibition.

OAKLEY, Juliana (d. after 1882)
Exh. PAFA, *Grapes*
The painting was owned by James L. Claghorn.

ORD, Joseph Biays (1805-1865)
(1832, second door from the corner of Third and Walnut;
1835, corner of Fifth and Minor St.; 1836, Philadelphia;
1837, 142 Chestnut St.; 1838-1847, 354 S. Front St.; 1849-
1850, 127 S. Front St.; 1854, 127 Front St.; 1856, 127 S. Front
St.; 1862, 784 S. Front St.)
Exh. PAFA, 1824 *Still Life – Peaches and Grapes* and *Still Life
– Oranges and Nuts;* 1827 *Oysters and Fruit,* stated to be after
Raphael (sic) Peale; 1838 *Peaches from Nature, Dudu after
Meadows,* and *Portrait of C. C. Biddle,* all owned by C. C.
Biddle; 1842 *Still Life – Temperance Picture* and *Still Life –
Peaches and Melon,* owned by W. G. Mason; 1843 *Still Life –
Peaches and Melon;* 1843 *Fruit and c,* owned by J. R.
Lambdin; 1845 *Still Life;* 1850 *Offerings to Bacchus – Still Life,
Composition;* 1856 *The Artist's Table,* Thomas M. Cash, and
*The Dentist's Table,* Dr. R. T. Reynolds.

He did not exhibit another still life until 1838, but concen-
trates on portraits and religious subjects and copies after
old masters. In 1838 and subsequent years Ord continued to exhibit regularly at PAFA. Mason, who owned *Still
Life – Peaches and Melon,* is probably the Philadelphia li-
thographer who worked with C. G. Childs on *Views of
Philadelphia from Original Views Taken in 1827-1830* and
with Joshua Shaw on *United States Architecture.* He exhibited a landscape at the PAFA in 1843. Another influence
on Ord may be inferred from his *Fruit & c* exhibited in
1843 and owned by J. R. Lambdin, father of G. C.
Lambdin. By 1845 the PAFA apparently already owned a
still life by this artist as it was exhibited in the exhibition
for that year and in subsequent years.

PAGON, Katharine Dunn
Exh. PAFA, 1918 *Still Life* cat. no. 150; 1919 *Still Life* cat.
no. 143; 1921 *Still Life* cat. no. 367

PEALE, Anna Claypoole (Mrs. William Staughton, 1791-
1878)
Anna Claypoole Peale, Margaretta Angelica (1795-1882)
and Sarah Miriam (1800-1885), all daughters of James
Peale, carried on the Philadelphia style of still life without great change.

PEALE, Charles Willson (1741-1827)
Probably the most interesting artist of Philadelphia, organizer of the first art school in America, portrait painter par excellence, and creator of the first American scientific museum, Charles Willson Peale was born in Maryland and served an apprenticeship as a saddler and woodcarver. He was the founder of the Philadelphia Peale family who for a century and more dominated artistic circles in that city.

PEALE, Harriet Cany (Mrs. Rembrandt, ca. 1800-1869)
The wife of Rembrandt Peale, Mrs. Harriet C. Peale lived in Philadelphia and Baltimore. Both before and after marriage, she exhibited portraits, still lifes, and copies at the Artists' Fund Society and the Pennsylvania Academy of the Fine Arts.

PEALE, James (1749-1831)
Born in Chestertown, MD, died in Philadelphia, PA
James Peale, brother of C. W. Peale, whose pupil he was, was born in Maryland. First a miniaturist and painter of conversation group portraits, he turned to still life in his old age. At least five of his seven children were known painters.

PEALE, Jr., James (1789-1876)
Son of James Peale, a painter of still lifes. He was a banker by profession and painted for pleasure. His two sons, Washington V. Peale, 1825-68 and James G. Peale, 1823-91 were painters of still lifes during their lifetimes.

PEALE, Margaretta Angelica (1795-1882)
Margaretta Angelica, Anna Claypoole, and Sarah Miriam (1800-1885), all daughters of James Peale, carried on the Philadelphia style of still life without great change.

PEALE, Maria (1787-1866)
A still life painter, Maria Peale, a daughter of James and a niece of Charles Willson Peale, was born in Philadelphia and spent virtually her entire life there.

PEALE, Mary Jane (1827-1902)
The daughter of Rubens Peale and granddaughter of Charles Willson Peale, Mary Jane Peale was an accomplished still life and portrait painter.

PEALE, Raphaelle (1774-1825)
Charles Willson Peale's eldest son, Raphaelle, was born in Annapolis, Maryland. He collaborated with his brother Rembrandt on many portraits and worked with his father at the Peale museum in Philadelphia. Later he cut silhouettes and turned to trompe-l'oeil paintings.

PEALE, Rembrandt (1778-1860)
Rembrandt Peale was the most celebrated son of the old master, Charles Willson Peale, and was born in Bucks County, Pa. He seemed to have much of the versatility of his father, and did portraits, miniatures, and historical subjects. He opened several scientific and artistic museums. His "Court of Death" is the only itinerant mural extant. His most famous work is his idealized portrait of George Washington, known as the "porthole," of which he painted 78 copies, changing Washington's garb in many. The finest example of this type, wearing a general's uniform, is in the Westmoreland Museum of Art collection. The National Gallery of Art, Washington, D.C., recently acquired Rembrandt's painting, *Rubens Peale with a Geranium*, 1801.

PEALE, Rubens (1784-1865)
Rubens Peale, born in Philadelphia, was the son of Charles Willson Peale. Because of weak eyesight, he did fewer paintings than other members of that talented and productive family, although a number of his still lifes and animal paintings are known.

PEALE, Sarah Miriam (1800-1885)
Sarah Miriam Peale, daughter of James Peale, is one of America's early professional female artists. She never married and supported herself for 60 years. She painted still lifes, but specialized in portraits.

PEALE, Titian Ramsay (1799-1885)
The son of Charles Willson Peale, Titian Ramsay was born in Philadelphia and is chiefly known as a naturalist and illustrator of works on natural history.

PETO, John Frederick (1854-1907)
Peto was born in Philadelphia and worked chiefly in that area, where his painting was so directly in the line of his friend W. M. Harnett's still lifes that many of his canvases were forged with the latter's signature and sold as genuine Harnetts. The fraud was not discovered until Alfred Frankenstein's study of still life, *After the Hunt*, appeared in 1953.

PIPPIN, Horace (1888-1946)
An unschooled black, native of West Chester, Pa., Pippin is a genuine primitive, innocent in spirit, colorful, and freshly charming. He began to paint after he was injured in a gas attack during World War I.

PLATT, G. W.
Exh. PAFA, 1878 *Fruit* cat. no. 176

PLATT, James C. (d. 1882)
  Exh. PAFA, *Fruit*, two belonging to Snedecor

PRATT, Matthew (1734-1805)
A native of Philadelphia, Pratt studied there under his uncle, James Claypoole. He painted portraits in Philadelphia and in New York for eight years before going to work with Benjamin West in London for four years, 1764-1768.

PRESSOIR, Esther Estelle
  Exh. PAFA, 1927 *Still Life* cat. no. 32

PREYER, Emilie (1849-1930)
  Exh. PAFA, *Fruit*, belonging to Claghorn

PREYER, Johann Wilhelm (1803-1889)
  Exh. PAFA, 1865 *Still Life*, for sale by Bailey & Co.; 1868 *Cherries and Nuts, Fruit*, drawing, and one other; two owned by Claghorn, one by Thomas A. Scott

RAMSEY, Milne (1847-1915)
  (1523 Chestnut St.; Haseltine Building, 1418 Chestnut, Philadelphia)
  Exh. PAFA, 1865, 1866, 1867, *Still Lifes*; 1885 *Study — Lilies* cat. no. 267; 1886 *Roses* cat. no. 212 and *Still Life* cat. no. 213; 1888 *Roses* cat. no. 262, *Grapes* cat. no. 263 and *Doughnuts* cat. no. 264; 1889 *Roses* cat. no. 183 and *Candlelight* cat. no. 184; 1890 *Le France Roses* cat. no. 163, *Nature Morte* cat. no. 165, *Peaches* cat. no. 166, *Smoked Herring* cat. no. 167 and *Chrysanthemums* cat. no. 168; *Attar (sic) of Roses* cat. no. 233 and *Still Life* cat. no. 235; 1892 *Still Life* cat. no. 195

Born in Philadelphia, he was a student at the Atelier Bonnat, Paris. He exhibited a still life at the 1868 Paris Salon and at the National Academy of Design and was also a painter of landscapes.

RAND, Harry A.
  Exh. PAFA, 1930 *Still Life* cat. no. 284

RANDLE, Fred
  Exh. PAFA, 1876 *Fruit* cat. no. 112

RAUGHT, John (1857-?)
  Exh. PAFA, 1885 *Still Life* cat. no. 268
Born in Scranton, he studied at the NAD.

READIO, Wilfred A. (1895-1961)
Born in Florence, Mass., he died in Pittsburgh, Pa. Wilfred A. Readio began his art studies under Alfred Vance Churchill in Northampton, Massachusetts. He continued under Arthur Watson Sparks at Carnegie Institute of Technology (now Carnegie-Mellon University) in Pittsburgh. His earlier, more impressionistic work is similar to Sparks'. "The Curtained Window," 1921, is

from that period and was awarded a first prize at the Associated Artists of Pittsburgh 1921 exhibition. He joined the Carnegie "Tech" faculty at age 24 and in 1939 he became head of the Department of Painting, Design and Sculpture — a position he held until 1955.

Although he was an able painter he preferred lithography and appreciated the full range of tones available in that medium. Aside from his Pittsburgh scenes, the American West held a special fascination for him and was the scene of his almost yearly summer sketching trips. Hallet's peak in the Colorado Rockies was one of his favorite sites.

REAM, Morston
  Exh. PAFA, 1876 *Peaches in Newspaper* cat. no. 9 and *Lady's Toilet* cat. no. 128

REICH, J.
  Exh. PAFA, 1878 *Fruit* cat. no. 209

REID, Mary Hiester (1854-?)
  (Yonge St., Arcade, Toronto, Canada)
  Exh. PAFA, 1891 *Panel: Roses* cat. no. 240; 1893 *Carnations* cat. no. 145
Born in Reading, PA, she studied at the PAFA and in Paris. She was a member of the Ontario Society of Artists.

RICHARDS, William Trost (1833-1900)

RIDDLE, Alice I.
  Exh. PAFA, 1915 *The Yellow Still Life* cat. no. 310

RIHL, Martha Landell (1863-?)
  (946 N. 8th St.; Care of Drexel, Harjes & Co., Paris)
  Exh. PAFA, 1887 *Apples and Cider* cat. no. 224 and *Wisteria* cat. no. 225; 1888 *Easter Lilies* cat. no. 280; 1891 *Still Life* cat. no. 149
She was born in Philadelphia.

ROBERTS, Ellent T.
  (Jenkintown, Montgomery Co., Pa.)
  Exh. PAFA, 1885 *Chrysanthemums* cat. no. 277 and *Roses* cat. no. 278
She studied at the PAFA.

ROBERTS, Rebekah Evens
  (1523 Chestnut St., Philadelphia)
  Exh. PAFA, 1886 *Still Life* cat. no. 229; 1888 *Study of Vegetables*; 1889 *Chrysanthemums* cat. no. 197
Born in New Jersey, she was a pupil of Milne Ramsey.

ROBIE, probably Jean Baptiste (1821-1910)
  Exh. PAFA, 1860 *Flowers and Grapes*, J. S. Earle & Son

ROESEN, Severin (active 1848-1871)
  Exh. PAFA, 1863 *Fruit Piece*, S. Swan, for sale

Born in Germany, Roesen came to this country about 1848, lived in Williamsport and in Philadelphia, where he died in an alms house. Most of his still lifes are owned in the neighborhood of Williamsport and he is often termed the "Williamsport painter."

ROOT, Orville Hoyt
> Exh. PAFA, 1914 *Still Life* cat. no. 155 and *Still Life* cat. no. 517

RUMLEY, Elizabeth (Mrs. B. Dawson)
In 1857, F. DeBourg Richards exhibited a still life by her at the PAFA.

SARAZIN, Mrs. L.
> (Hamilton Village artist)
> Exh. PAFA, 1822 *Vase of Flowers and Fruit*; 1827 *A Basket of Flowers with Fruit*, painted in oil on velvet

SCATTERGOOD, Mary P. (1864-?)
> (1511 Oxford St., Philadelphia)
> Exh. PAFA, 1888 *Still Life — Herring* cat. no. 297
Born in Philadelphia, she studied at the School of Design for Women.

SCHETKY, Caroline (Mrs. Samuel Richardson, ca. 1790-1852)
> (Various addresses on Locust St., Philadelphia)
> Exh. PAFA, 1818 *Wild Geranium — From Nature*
Schetky was exhibiting large numbers of miniature paintings in the years 1818-1826. The geranium seems to have been an exceptional picture for her.

SCHEYER, W. H.
> (16th & Tioga, Philadelphia)
> Exh. PAFA, 1886 *Still Life* cat. no. 242
Born in Philadelphia, the artist studied at PAFA.

SCOTT, Jannette
> Exh. PAFA, 1886 *Chrysanthemums* cat. no. 244
She was a student at PAFA.

SEARS, Helen W. (1865-?)
> (1920 Mt. Vernon St., Philadelphia)
> Exh. PAFA, 1885 *Panel of Bennett and Sunset Roses* cat. no. 294
Born in New York City, she studied at PAFA, and with J. Liberty Tadd.

SELIGMAN, Mrs. Emma
> (1348 Spruce St., Philadelphia)
> Exh. PAFA, 1862-1867 Many *Still Lifes of Fruit, Grapes*, often the property of Henry Seligman; 1867 *Under-graduate Orioles*

SELLERS, Anna (1824-1905)
> Exh. PAFA, *Still Life of Peaches*
This painting depicts two peaches on a polished table top and was on the New York art market in 1981; inscribed "Painted by Anna Sellers niece of Rembrandt Peale in the year 1861/Owned by Henrietta Frances Griscome Parsons. Cousin of Anna Rielly of Haddonfield and Grace Parsons Wilkinson."

SHAMBERG, Morton Livingston (1881-1918)

SHEELER, Charles (1883-1965)
> Exh. PAFA, 1930 *Still Life* cat. no. 282
Born in Philadelphia, Sheeler studied at the Pennsylvania Academy and later became interested in various experimental methods in painting.

He is famous as a photographer and a painter, and began his studies in Philadelphia in the School of Industrial Art. After attending the Pennsylvania Academy of the Fine Arts, he traveled in Europe. He was an important member of the precisionist movement. Sheeler died in Hobbs Ferry, New York.

SHEPPARD, Fannie
> (2019 Arch St., Philadelphia)
> Exh. PAFA, 1885 *Azaleas* cat. no. 300
Born in Philadelphia.

SHIBE, Mrs.
> Exh. PAFA, 1837 *Still Life*, watercolor

SINNICKSON, Mary H.
> (2319 De Lancey Place, Philadelphia)
> Exh. PAFA, 1886 *Study of Marigolds* cat. no. 260
Born in Philadelphia, she studied at PAFA, and with William Sartain.

SITER, Eliza C.
> (2033 Locust St., Philadelphia)
> Exh. PAFA, 1885 *Azaleas* cat. no. 314 and *Peonies* cat. no. 315
Born in Philadelphia, she studied at the PAFA.

SLOAN, John

SMITH, Esther Morton (1865-?)
> (4717 Germantown Ave., Philadelphia)
> Exh. PAFA, 1889 *Still Life* cat. no. 209; 1891 *Sketch of Nasturtiums* cat. no. 276
She was born in Germantown, Philadelphia.

SMITH, Mary (1842-1878)
> (Jenkinson, Pa.)
Mrs. Smith sent her standard chicken and animal paintings to PAFA annually. In 1865, she sent *The Balsam Apple*, most likely a chick with an apple, and not a pure still life.

SMITH, Thomas Henry
(Philadelphia)
Exh. PAFA, 1863 *Peach and Grapes,* for sale

SMITH, W.
Exh. PAFA, 1819 *Still Life—Grapes* and *Still Life—Peaches*

SMITH, Mrs. William T. Russell (Mary Priscilla Wilson)
(Jenkintown)
Exh. PAFA, 1862 *Study of Flowers*

SMITH, Xanthus (1838-1929)
Exh. PAFA, 1862 *Wild Strawberries,* property of Miss M. Smith; *Still Life of Fruit and Nuts on the Ground* sold at the Shute Auction Gallery, Bridgewater, Mass., April 26, 1987.

SNYDERS, Frans (1579-1657)
Exh. PAFA, 1811 *Fruit Piece*

SPENCER, Margaret Fulton
Exh. PAFA, 1916 *Still Life, The Brown Jar* cat. no. 201; 1917 *Still Life, Mandarin Bowl* cat. no. 52 and *Still Life, Green and Gold,* cat. no. 114; 1918 *The Red Jar* cat. no. 375; 1919 *Asters* cat. no. 269; 1921 *Still Life with Fruit* cat. no. 160 and *Blue, Tan and Violet* cat. no. 334; 1922 *Flowers* cat. no. 334; 1926 *Button Chrysanthemums* cat. no. 26; 1927 *Winter Bouquet* cat. no. 275; 1929 *Summer Flowers* cat. no. 10 and *Petunias and Phlox* cat. no. 13

STEHLIN, Caroline
Exh. PAFA, 1905 *Still Life* cat. no. 470

STODDARD, Alice Kent
Exh. PAFA, 1913 *Poppies* cat. no. 224

STREET, Robert (1796-1865)
Born in Germantown, Pennsylvania, a versatile artist of mid-century who attempted history and religious painting, landscape and still life paintings, as well as portraiture which was his stock and trade. In 1859 he exhibited *Still Life (fruit),* the property of Rev. John Street, at the PAFA, where he had begun to exhibit regularly in 1815. In addition to being an artist, Street was a collector of Old Master paintings, owning examples attributed to Annibale Carracci, Anthony Van Dyck. Street was married three times and like Charles Willson Peale allowed his admiration for the masters to influence his choice of his children's names: Austin, Del Sarto, Rubens, Correggio, and Claude Lorraine, all of whom became artists, but none successful. In 1840 Street held an exhibition of 172 of his paintings at the Artists' Fund Hall along with fifty examples from his collection of "Old Masters." The notes to the Street catalogue do not mention still life painting, but praise his skill and success "in numerous instances of portraiture, of the most difficult kind from the corpse."

STROUD, Laura D. (1863-?)
(2035 Mt. Vernon, Philadelphia)
Exh. PAFA, 1889 *Still Life* cat. no. 219
Born in Philadelphia, she studied at PAFA.

SWORD, J. B.
Exh. PAFA, 1878 *Still Life—Quail* cat. no. 263 and *Still Life—Woodcock* cat. no. 304

TALMAN, John
Pupil of Roesen in Williamsport.

TANNER, Juliet L.
(1508 Chestnut St., Philadelphia)
Exh. PAFA, 1886 *Jar of Chrysanthemums* cat. no. 279

TAYLOR, Charles Jay (1885-1929)
Born in Greenwich Village, New York City, Charles Jay Taylor was head of the Painting and Decoration Department in the College of Fine Arts at the Carnegie Institute of Technology, now known as Carnegie-Mellon University, Pittsburgh, at the time of his death in 1929.

He occupied a definite place in the field of art and was nationally known as an illustrator and a painter. In the earlier days of his career, he lent his talents to black and white and he was one of the best illustrators of the gay-nineties' miss, as shown by his famous Taylor-made Girl, who was perhaps a harbinger of the later Gibson Girl. H. C. Bunner's "Short Sixes" and "More Short Sixes," which first appeared in "Puck," are probably the most familiar of the sketches which he illustrated. He did these with such interpretative sympathy that he shared honors with Bunner.

With the passing of the years, his artistic genius turned to the mellower medium of oils, with landscapes his favorite subject, and here again he achieved a notable success.

Taylor had exhibited paintings in the International Exhibitions of the Carnegie Institute and the exhibitions of the Associated Artists of Pittsburgh. He received honorable mention at the Pan-American Association, was Hors Concour at the Panama Pacific Exposition and also received a medal for distinguished services.

TAYLOR, Margaret M.
(1529 N. Seventeenth St., Philadelphia)
Exh. PAFA, 1885 *Herring* cat. no. 334; 1886 *Ducks* cat. no. 280
Born in Philadelphia, she studied at the School of Design for Women.

THIBAULT, Miss C. (Aimee, 1780-1868)
Exh. PAFA, 1814 *Flowers*

THOMAS, J. Stirling
Exh. PAFA, 1876 *Still Life* cat. no. 108

THOMAS, Joseph S.
(651 North 11th St., Philadelphia)
Exh. PAFA, 1865 *Fruit*

THOMAS, Paul K. M.
(514 Walnut St., Philadelphia)
Exh. PAFA, 1900 *Chrysanthemums* cat. no. 43 and *Roses* cat. no. 238

THOMASON, Frances Q.
Exh. PAFA, 1905 *Still Life* cat. no. 360

TORREY, Hiram Dwight (1820-1900)
Exh. PAFA, 1855 *Still Life, Peaches*
Born in New Lebanon, N.Y. After his first marriage in 1851, he was active in Milwaukee, Wis., later moving to Reading, Pa., from 1853 until 1862. In that year he moved his family to Glascow, Scotland, where a son was born in 1870. Torrey died in Delanco, N. J.

TORREY, Juliette E.
(229 Arch St., Philadelphia)
Exh. PAFA, 1832 *Basket of Fruit*

TOWNE, Rosalba (Rosa) M. (1827-1909)
(1860, 810 Chestnut St.; 1861, 1426 Pine St.; 1862-65, 816 Chestnut St.; 1866 Pine St.; 1868-69, Shoemakertown, Pa. Exh. PAFA, *Still Lifes of Exotic Flowers*; 1860, *Indian Bloodroot*; 1861, *Newport Autumn Flowers, Mountain Summer Flowers*; 1862, *The Bird's Nest*, belonging to J. H. Towne; 1865, *Spring in the City* and *Spring in the Country*; 1869, *Calla Lily*, and *Poinsetta*, and *Adder Tongue Lily Trillion* offered for sale by James S. Earle.
Daughter of John and Sarah Robertson Towne and sister of the artist, Ann Sofia Towne Darragh, she was a flower and landscape painter and a botanical illustrator. The Harvard Botanical Museum has examples of her work. She lived in Pittsburgh from 1833-40 and also 1840-51; Philadelphia, 1860-66; and Shoemaker, Pa., 1868-69, the years she exhibited at the Pennsylvania Academy of the Fine Arts.

TSCHERING, Miss Anthonie
Exh. PAFA, 1876 *Alpine Roses* cat. no. 153

UHLE, B.
Exh. PAFA, *Still Life—Game* cat. no. 206

VALLAYER-COSTER, Anne (1744-1818)
Exh. PAFA, 1856 *Flower Piece in Miniature*

VAN DEN WARDEN
Exh. PAFA, 1865 *Fruit and Flowers* (W. Sellers)

VAN TRUMP, Rebecca
(1520 Chestnut St., Philadelphia)

Exh. PAFA, 1893 *Chrysanthemums* cat. no. 155
Studied at PAFA.

VON HELMBOLD, Adele M.
(1710 Chestnut St., Philadelphia)
Exh. PAFA, 1895 *Roses* cat. no. 336

WALL, Alfred Bryan (1861-1935)
A lifelong resident of the Pittsburgh area, Wall was the son of noted landscape painter Alfred S. Wall and a nephew of William Coventry Wall from whom he received his artistic training. His work was exhibited at the NAD in 1879. Later he maintained a studio in Philadelphia. He served as a trustee of the Carnegie Institute from its inception in 1896 and was also a member of the Fine Arts Committee which helped to select the permanent collection. Best known for his domestic scenes, often of local shepherds painted in a Barbizon influenced manner. He painted several still lifes of hanging fish in the trompe l'oeil manner.

WASHBURN, Cadwallader
Exh. PAFA, 1907 *Still Life* cat. no. 116

WATSON, Elizabeth H.
(162 N. 20th St., Philadelphia)
Exh. PAFA, 1886 *Study of Daisies* cat. no. 306; 1888 *Chrysanthemums* cat. no. 352
She studied at PAFA, and under William Sartain.

WAUGH, Amy
(4100 Pine St., Philadelphia)
Exh. PAFA, 1885 *Still Life Study* cat. no. 357
She was born in Philadelphia.

WAY, A. J.
Exh. PAFA, 1878 *California Grapes—Flamme de Tokay* cat. no. 201; *On the Half Shell* cat. no. 240

WEEKS, Miss E. A.
(544 North 4th St., Philadelphia)
Exh. PAFA, 1868 *Strawberries*

WELFARE, Daniel C. (1796-1841)
Exh. PAFA, 1825 *Still Life—Apples, Oranges, Wine*
Born in North Carolina, he was a student of Thomas Sully at the PAFA in 1825. He died in Salem, North Carolina. Welfare named his son after Sully, who in turn is said to have painted a self-portrait for his namesake.

WELLS, H. M.
Exh. PAFA, 1821 *Basket of Flowers*, painted on velvet

WERNER, Martin
(1020 Ridge Ave., Philadelphia)

Exh. PAFA, 1865 *Fruit*

He also exhibited a genre painting.

WEST, William Edward (1788-1857)
(1817, 110 N. 4th St., Philadelphia; 1827-1829, 32 N. 4th St.,
Philadelphia; 1832, 115 Arch St., London)
Exh. PAFA, 1827 *Still-Life—Barrel and Jug*

WILKINSON, Mrs. Ella Foster (1855-?)
(1617 Arch St., Philadelphia)
Exh. PAFA, 1885 *Peonies* cat. no. 370

She was born in Danville, Pa.

WILLIAMS, Mary
Exh. PAFA, 1811 *Basket of Flowers;* 1814 *Fruit*

WILLIAMSON
Exh. PAFA, 1867 *Prize Tuberose,* Mrs. J. Notman

WILLOUGHBY, Annie (1855-?)
(1433 Norris St., Philadelphia)
Exh. PAFA, 1886 *California Grapes* cat. no. 319 and *Chrysanthemums* cat. no. 320

Born in Philadelphia, she studied at the Philadelphia
School of Design for Women under George C. Lambdin.

WILSON, Alexander (1766-1813)

WISE, Ella G.
(2023 Mt. Vernon St., Philadelphia)
Exh. PAFA, 1888 *Study of Pipe and Tobacco* cat. no. 369

Born in Philadelphia, she was a pupil of Milne Ramsey.

WISE, Ellie S.
(2023 Mt. Vernon St., Philadelphia)
Exh. PAFA, 1886 *Chrysanthemums* cat. no. 321 and *Roses* cat.
no. 322

She was a pupil of Milne Ramsey.

WOOD, Jr., George Bacon (1832-1909)
Exh. PAFA, 1864, *Callas Lilies*

Born into a Quaker family in Philadelphia, Wood studied
at the PAFA and possibly saw the American exhibition of
British Art when it was shown in February 1858. Seems
to have been following W. T. Richards in his landscape
paintings; showed *Natural Bridge, Va.* at the PAFA in 1859.

WOODSIDE, Abraham (1819-1853)
Son of John Archibald and painted still lifes very much
like his father.

WOODSIDE, John Archibald Sr., (1781-1852)
(1829-1830, 61 S. 5th St.; 1834, N. St. above 5th; 1836, 30 N.
St., Philadelphia)
Exh. PAFA, 1821 *Still Life—Apples, Peaches, Grapes* and *Still

Life—Apples, Pears, Peaches, and Grapes;* 1829, *Peaches and
Grapes, Peaches,* and *Dead Game,* property of W. H. Strick-
land until 1853 and in 1859 was the property of F. DeBurg
Richards; 1831, *Fruit Pieces;* 1834, *Portrait of a Dog, Dead
Game, and Grapes.*

Born in Philadelphia, Woodside was immortalized by
William Dunlap in his HRPAD as an artist who "paints
signs with talent beyond many who paint in the higher
branches," a quotation repeated by almost all who chron-
icled the arts in Philadelphia when he died at age 71. The
Public Ledger (February 28, 1852) said "he was one of the
best sign-painters in the State, and perhaps in the country, and was the first to raise this branch of art to the de-
gree of excellence here, which is now attained." This
notoriety was well deserved in that paintings by the artist
which have been discovered in recent years are indeed
better than one would expect from a sign painter. Woodside's early training was with Matthew Pratt or one associated with him. Early in his career in June 1802, he was
associated with William Berrett, a coach and sign painter.
By 1803 he opened his own establishment where he
painted fire buckets and regimental colors for several out-
lying Pennsylvania counties. Many of his still lifes are lin-
ear and high in color, a hold over from his work in the
oranmental line. His best work of the period compares
favorably with the work of James Peale. At the PAFA he
was a frequent exhibitor of still lifes and animals. The
PAFA owns a still life of a *Dead Rabbit.* He also was re-
sponsible for decorating drums and parade banners, but
was best known for his decorations for Philadelphia's
volunteer fire companies, for whom he painted banners,
buckets, capes, and hats, as well as panels for the sides of
their prized hose carriages and engines. Woodside's rep-
utation as an ornamental painter eventually spread as far
as New York where he was commissioned to paint fire
engine boards.

WOOSTER, Austin C. (1864-1913)
active Pittsburgh, 1864-1913

Little is known of Wooster's life or background. He was
born in Chartiers Valley, near Pittsburgh, and died in
Pittsburgh. During the Civil War he served with the Union Army, was captured and held at Libby Prison. Except
for that episode in his life, he is thought to have lived and
worked exclusively in this region. Earlier in his career he
painted landscapes, especially river scenes, but later
turned to still life utilizing much of the same style and
compositional devices as Albert F. King, an artist whom
Wooster obviously admired and possibly even "went to
for instruction."

WYDEVELDE, Arnoud
(New York)
Exh. PAFA, 1862 *Fruit*

WYETH, Newell Convers (1882-1945)

Born in Needham, Mass. and died in Chadds Ford, Pa.

Wyeth, a popular illustrator for such children's classics as Robert Louis Stevenson's *Treasure Island* and James Fenimore Cooper's *The Last of the Mohicans,* studied with Howard Pyle at Chadds Ford and worked for the *Saturday Evening Post.*

He is perhaps more notable as the founder of what has become the successful painting dynasty. Three of his five children became painters. Henriette married the painter, Peter Hurd, and without a doubt the best known artist in America today is his son, Andrew Wyeth, whose son Jamie has reached a remarkable point in his career.

ZOGBAUM, Helene
> (1020 Chestnut, Philadelphia)
> Exh. PAFA, 1890 *Still Life* cat. no. 237 and *Chrysanthemums* cat. no. 238; 1891 *Still Life* cat. no. 337

She studied at the PAFA.

TYPOGRAPHY: Set in Palacio types
by Chas. M. Henry Printing Co.
COLOR SEPARATIONS: Chas. M. Henry Printing Co.
and Kreber Graphics
PRINTING: Chas. M. Henry Printing Co.
BINDING: Chas. M. Henry Printing Co.
PAPER: S. D. Warren Co. — Lustro Dull Enamel — Basis 80#